DISCOVERING CABOT'S BRISTOL

discovering
CABOT'S BRISTOL

Life in the Medieval and Tudor Town

Peter Fleming
& Kieran Costello

In association with

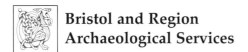

First published in 1998 by Redcliffe Press

ISBN 1 900178 51 6

British Library Cataloguing-in-Publication-Data
A CIP data for this book is available from the British Library

Cover picture: Hoefnagle's plan of Bristol, 1581 (© Bristol City Museum)

REDCLIFFE PRESS
Halsgrove House
Lower Moor Way
Tiverton EX16 6SS
T: 01884 243242
F: 01884 243325
www.halsgrove.com

Printed and bound in Great Britain
by WBC Ltd, Bridgend

CONTENTS

ACKNOWLEDGEMENTS

We should like to thank John Burton, Ann Rippin, and Professor Geoffrey Channon and the Faculty of Humanities at the University of the West of England, for their generous help, encouragement and advice. This book also owes much to the advice and financial assistance provided by Bruce Williams and the Bristol and Region Archaeological Services, whose work has done so much to elucidate Bristol's medieval past.

Photographs are reproduced by kind permission of the following:

Bristol City Museum (CM); Bristol Record Office (BRO); the Diocese of Bristol (DB); the Central Reference Library (CRL); the church of St Mary Redcliffe (StMR); St Thomas's church (StThom); St Stephen's church (StSteph); the National Health Service (NHS).

PREFACE

There is no doubting Bristol's place in British history. From its roots as a stronghold on the frontier between the English and the Welsh, through its medieval growth as the major west-coast port to become the realm's greatest town after London, its eighteenth-century 'golden age' – whose prosperity owed so much to the appalling trade in African slaves – to its modern associations with cutting-edge technology (whether in nineteenth-century railways or twentieth-century aerospace), Bristol's constantly changing character has often put it at the forefront of the nation's story.

This splendidly illustrated book explores a time when the foundations were laid of so much of Bristol's modern development. During the 170 years from the 1370s to 1540s, 'Cabot's Bristol' began to look towards the Atlantic, while its political and commercial importance was recognised when it became the first provincial town to be granted county status. We take particular pleasure in being associated with this book, since this period saw not only the origins of the City and County of Bristol – a status recently restored after the abolition of the County of Avon – but also the beginnings of that tradition of educational excellence of which the University of the West of England is proud to be a part.

Alfred Morris,
Vice Chancellor,
The University of the West of England

The Rt Hon. The Lord Mayor Of Bristol,
Councillor Jack Fisk OBE

INTRODUCTION

*L*ater medieval and early Tudor Bristol is famous as the port from which John Cabot embarked in 1497 on his historic voyage to Newfoundland. John Cabot is certainly Bristol's best-known resident from this period, even though he spent only a few years in the town. However, Bristol was much more than just a convenient point of departure for Atlantic explorers. From the late 1300s to the early 1500s Bristol was England's third greatest town, only surpassed in population and wealth by London and York. This book explores this fascinating community, and creates a picture of what Cabot would have seen during his short stay.

This is the story of Bristol from the 1370s to the early 1540s, a time and a place we have called 'Cabot's Bristol'. While John Cabot disappeared at sea in 1498, his son, Sebastian, lived on into the middle of the next century, and maintained his links with Bristol, so in this sense even at the end of our period the town is still 'Cabot's Bristol'. On the other hand, we can only understand how the town had developed into the Bristol the Cabots knew by looking further back into its history, as far as the later fourteenth century.

This is also the story of the Town and County of Bristol. In 1373 Bristol became the first English town outside London to be granted county status: henceforth, it enjoyed legal independence from the counties of Gloucestershire and Somerset which surrounded it. This event gives us our starting point. Our finishing point is provided by the creation of the

This engraving of Sebastian Cabot in later life (he died in 1557) is from a lost, reputedly contemporary portrait. (© CM)

9

Diocese of Bristol, in 1542. By this act Bristol acquired its own cathedral and was thereby elevated from Town to Cathedral City.

This is a particularly colourful period in English history, and the backdrop to Bristol's story is provided by greater dramas made familiar to us by Shakespeare: the Hundred Years War; the deposition of Richard II in 1399; Henry V's victory at Agincourt; the loss of England's French possessions under Henry VI; the Wars of the Roses; the death of Richard III and the establishment of the Tudor dynasty in 1485, and the Reformation under Henry VIII. All of these national events, and many more, had their impact on Bristol.

The book is divided into two sections. The first tells the story of later medieval and early Tudor Bristol, from 1373 to 1542, in terms of the major themes of the economy, politics, society and religion. This story can be told in some detail thanks to Bristol's magnificent archives. The second section is made up of three walking tours which enable us to explore what can still be seen of 'Cabot's Bristol': despite the depredations of centuries, there is still an astonishingly rich medieval and early Tudor heritage. Much of the background evidence for these walks comes from two sources. The first is a detailed description of the town, written by William Worcestre, a scholarly antiquarian who can probably be called England's first local historian. Worcestre was born in Bristol in 1415 (the same year as the Battle of Agincourt), and as an old man he paced around the town's streets, carefully measuring and noting what he saw. The second source is the large body of evidence which has resulted from many years of archaeological excavation.

CLOTH AND CANVAS

A late fourteenth-century stonemason, looking northwards from the tower of St Mary
Redcliffe on which he was working, could
see at a glance the twin foundations of Bristol's prosperity. Spread out below him were the dye works
and tenter racks of the Redcliffe and Temple Fee
cloth workers; beyond, a forest of masts and canvas
floating on the shimmering Avon, lay the ships of the
port's wealthy merchants.

One of the mainstays of Bristol's overseas trade
was the importation of luxury goods. These came
mainly from, or were supplied through, southern
Europe. Foremost among these luxuries was wine.

Wine was a major status symbol. It had to be
imported, since the vineyards the Romans had
planted in south-east England had long been abandoned, and was therefore expensive, and so then as
now it was considered a more refined tipple than ale,
the drink of the masses. In 1152 England acquired
Gascony, and with it a guaranteed supply of French
wine. Gascon wine, shipped from Bordeaux, was a
major element in Bristol's economy. In 1386–7, for
example, Bristol accounted for about one-tenth of
England's total wine imports. Only London, Sand-
wich and Southampton imported more wine than
Bristol.

This was not an easy trade. Mariners on the
Bordeaux–Bristol run had always faced the dangers
of storm and shipwreck, particularly since these
were autumn and winter voyages (after the vintage
had been harvested). Wrecks were considered fair

The chapel of the Virgin Mary, in the north porch of St Mary Redcliffe; the arches display oriental influences. Sailors are said to have come to this chapel to pray before embarking on perilous voyages. (© StMR, DB)

game by coastal dwellers: in the 1390s the crew of a
Bristol ship wrecked in the Severn Channel was
forcibly prevented from salvaging the vessel by the
locals, who then went on to strip and dismantle it.
Piracy was another constant threat, and French,
Italian and Spanish pirates were a particular

problem: in the autumn of 1400, for example, seven Bristol ships were captured by Spanish pirates. In order to recoup their losses, victims of piracy were often licensed by the crown to prey on the pirates' compatriots, which further exacerbated the situation. There was always a ready market for wine, and so it was especially prized by pirates and wreckers. Captured merchants could also be held to ransom: this was the experience of Thomas Canynges, nephew of William, whose lands had to be mortgaged to raise the £100 demanded by his Breton captors.

After the outbreak of the Hundred Years War with France in 1337 there was the additional danger of enemy action. Protection could sometimes be had from royal men-of-war, but for the most part the Bristol wine fleet had to fend for itself, organising convoys and carrying twice the normal crew, heavily armed to repel boarders. All of this made wine more scarce and expensive, but as long as Gascony remained an English possession the risks were well worth taking, and reasonable profits could be made.

Disaster struck in 1453: a devastating French offensive left only Calais and the Channel Islands in English hands. The French wine trade did not collapse – Gascony's economy was too dependent on the English market for its new masters to impose a total embargo – but henceforth English merchants were made very aware that they were dealing with the enemy: costly licences and safe conducts had to be purchased, and to the traditional dangers of capture at sea was added the threat of the confiscation of their cargoes in French ports.

Bristol wine merchants saw the wisdom of developing links with other suppliers. Foremost among these were the Portuguese and the Spanish. Wine from the Iberian Peninsula such as malmsey, romeney, osey, and a Portuguese sweet white wine with the unlikely name of bastard, was popular in England, and Bristol was already importing small quantities before the loss of Gascony. After 1453, while French wine continued to make up the bulk of Bristol's wine imports, the Spanish and Portuguese trade became increasingly significant. By 1500, Spain supplied one-third of Bristol's wine imports. While the large-scale importation of sherry was to begin only in the later sixteenth century, the famous association between Bristol and Iberian wine originated in the age of Cabot.

Wine was not the only commodity that crossed the Bay of Biscay. To Bristol came Gascon woad, used for dyeing cloth, as well as Spanish and Portuguese iron, olive oil, wax, fruit, honey, almonds, licorice, saffron,

Common seal of the Bristol burgesses, c. 1300. The Latin inscription reads: 'I am the key of the port.' (© BRO)

vinegar, soap, beaver fur, salt and dyestuffs. Portugal also supplied cork and Madeira sugar. That this does not exhaust the list of Iberian imports can be seen by a visit to the Lord Mayor's Chapel. Here, in the Poyntz Chantry, are ceramic floor tiles which were brought back from Spain in the 1530s. In return for these exotic southern goods, Bristol sent tanned hides, lead, tin, and alabaster sculptures of saints; but above all, Bristol dressed the Spanish and the Portuguese with English cloth. By the 1490s, over half of Bristol's cloth exports went to Spain.

While most Bristol merchants were content to diversify only as far as the Atlantic coasts of Spain and Portugal, some looked further, and were willing to risk lives and fortunes in forbidden and uncharted seas. From beyond the Straits of Gibraltar came the most exotic goods of all: spices, silks and other luxuries from the semi-mythical lands of the East. However, the Mediterranean had been a firm monopoly of the Italians, who sold these tantalising commodities in England while Bristol merchants could only look on and wonder. But in the middle of the fifteenth century the Venetian hold on Egypt was slipping, and this, combined with the loss of Gascony, prompted the Bristol merchant Robert Sturmy to take the risk. In 1458–9 Sturmy sailed with three ships into the Mediterranean to exchange cloth, wool, tin, lead and dye for spices and green peppers, but several Genoese ships attacked them off Malta and stole their cargoes. Sturmy himself may not have survived the engagement. When news of this reached Bristol, the mayor petitioned the king for action, and as a result all the Genoese merchants in London were imprisoned until they had paid the enormous sum of £6000 in compensation.

By contrast, the freezing waters of the far north offered their own share of adventure and wealth. By the early fifteenth century Bristol's share of the Icelandic trade was greater than any other English port. The attraction of this island on the edge of the known world was its vast fishing grounds. In return, the Icelanders were eager not only for basic necessities, including household goods, iron, vinegar and salt, but also for luxuries such as almonds. Bristol's great demand for fish is explained by the restrictions medieval Christianity imposed on the eating of meat. During Lent (the forty days before Easter), on Fridays and some feast days meat could not be eaten, and fish in bewildering variety was substituted. Most fish was salted, or dried (stockfish).

Of Iceland to write is little need,
Save of stockfish; yet for sooth indeed,
Out of Bristol, and coasts many one,
Men have practised by needle and by stone,
Thither-wards within a little while,
Gone and come, as men were wont of old,
Of Scarborough unto the coasts cold.
(*The Libelle of Englysh Polycye*, 15th century)

Bristol merchants also dealt in human cargoes: not slaves, but pilgrims. Before the mid-fifteenth century Bristol was a favourite point of embarkation for pilgrims bound for the great shrine of St James at Santiago de Compostela in Spain. A few went even further, to the greatest shrine of all, the Holy Sepulchre at Jerusalem; this was a long and perilous journey. William Worcestre tells of one such voyage that ended in disaster. In 1446 Robert Sturmy sent his ship *Anne* to the Holy Land with 160 pilgrims; on its return journey, two days before Christmas, the ship was hit by a great storm and broke up at night on rocks close to the port of Modon in Greece. Thirty-seven pilgrims and sailors were drowned, 'to the great sorrow of their friends and wives in Bristol', but the bishop of Modon gave them honorable burial, and built a chapel to their memory.

Trade with the continent was the means by which great fortunes were made and lost. But these ventures across the seas were not the staple element in the port's economy. More prosaic, but probably more important to Bristol's commercial health, was the trade with Ireland, Wales, and along the coasts and rivers of the South West of England. Bristol was superbly positioned for this trade. Down the Severn came grain and wool from Gloucestershire, Worcestershire and Herefordshire. From the South Wales coast and down the Wye through Chepstow came iron and timber from the Forest of Dean, wool, hides for the Bristol leather industry, and an inexpensive, poor-quality russet cloth popular with those who wanted a place in Heaven on the cheap by giving clothes to the poor in return for their prayers. From the South West came Somerset cloth, together with fish and tin from Devon and Cornwall.

Ireland was at least nominally under English rule, and provided large numbers of hides, and fish in enormous quantities. Less significant were Irish linen and cloth. Bristol's major exports to Ireland were cloth, as well as exotic items of the Iberian trade: iron, grain, salt (to preserve fish), vinegar, and of course, wine.

> Herring of Sligo and salmon of Bann, has made in Bristol many a rich man.
>
> (Local proverb)

The example of William Canynges, Bristol's most famous, and probably best-documented, merchant, provides an insight into the commercial life of the fifteenth-century port, but he was far from being the 'typical' Bristol merchant: he is famous largely because of the unusual scale of his operations, which brought forth abundant comment from contemporaries and subsequent generations. William was born into a family of cloth makers and exporters in 1402. By 1436 he was sending his own ship abroad, laden with cloth. But there is no indication that this was his own cloth: rather, he had decided to specialise as a shipowner and merchant; cloth production he left to others. In the fourteenth century it was general practice for cloth producers to ship their produce themselves; in William's lifetime the shipping and selling of cloth was increasingly the preserve of specialised merchants, and ship-owning also became a distinct profession. By the end of the fifteenth century there had emerged an elite of shipowners who made the bulk of their profits from leasing their ships to merchants.

William Worcestre tells us that William Canynges had ten ships, including the *Mary Redcliffe* of 500 tons, the *Mary Canynges* (perhaps named after a daughter), and the mighty 900-ton *Mary and John*, which cost over £2666 to build.

> Master William Canynges who was mayor ... five times in eight years kept 800 men employed in maritime occupations, and every day had labourers, masons and carpenters, etc. to the number of 100 men.
>
> (William Worcestre)

Worcestre's figures for the Canynges fleet appear to be born out by customs records, and would mean that William owned nearly half of Bristol's ships. But most ships were owned by groups of ship-owners, to spread the risks. The need to cover losses, and the great demand created by a shortage of vessels, made

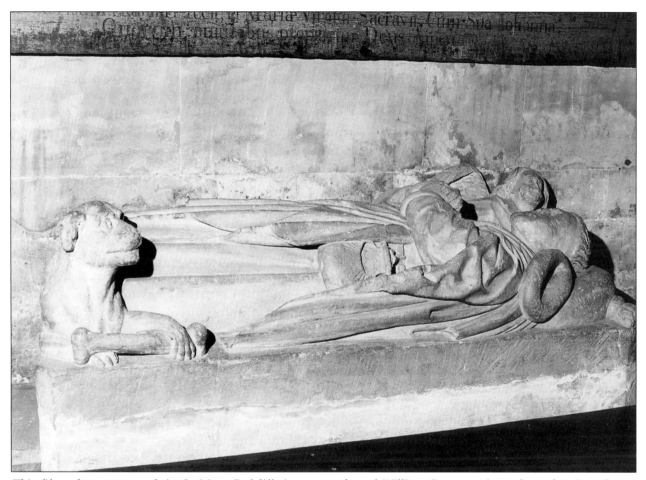

This fifteenth-century tomb in St Mary Redcliffe is next to that of William Canynges (see colour plates), and may commemorate his almoner or secretary. (© StMR)

the hire of ships an expensive business: for the shipment of wine, the ship owner would usually charge one sixth of the price the cargo would bring in England. In one year at the height of his career William may have received as much as £10,000 in freight charges, but half of this could be wiped out with the loss of just one large ship and its cargo.

William traded with Prussia and Dantzig, and he lost a ship on the Iceland run, but in common with most of the merchant elite the bulk of his trade was

15

probably with Gascony and Iberia. However, this latter trade was not the sole preserve of the elite: in 1479/80, 250 Bristolians traded with Gascony, Spain and Portugal. Among the wider group of lesser traders were sailors, who used their portage allowance to trade in the odd bale of cloth or barrel of wine.

Merchants spread the risks by distributing their cargoes between several ships. Merchants' marks were used to distinguish individual cargoes. These were legally recognised, and like the heraldry of the nobles and gentry were sometimes displayed on their owners' tombs.

By the late fourteenth century, nearly a quarter of Bristol's population was directly dependent on the cloth industry, concentrated in the suburbs of Redcliffe and Temple Fee. In the fourteenth century Bristol was the greatest cloth-exporting town in England, and only Salisbury was a larger cloth producer. However, Bristol's pre-eminence as a cloth exporter did not last beyond 1400: Bristol was outpaced by London at the beginning of the fifteenth century and by Exeter at its end. Bristol's position as a cloth producer, moreover, declined at a far more alarming rate.

Cloth making was a long process, involving several different specialised crafts with their own guilds. After the wool had been combed or carded (to open out and separate the wool) and spun into yarn (increasingly on a spinning wheel rather than the traditional distaff: spinning, like carding, was a female preserve, hence the term 'spinster'), it was woven on looms. Weaving was done by both sexes, but only men could be members of the Weavers' Guild. Guild ordinances demanded that looms should only be set up in ground-floor rooms open to the street, and that weaving should only take place in daylight, so that the quality of the work could be readily inspected. After weaving the cloth was fulled. Fulling 'felted' the cloth, knitting together the fibres to produce a denser fabric, but first the impurities had to be removed by washing with fuller's

Merchants' marks, their equivalent of coats of arms, indicated ownership of cargoes and other property. Shown here are the marks of: John Jay (d. c. 1480); John Barstaple (d. 1411) and Thomas Rowley (d. 1478). (© CM)

The tomb of Edmund Blanket and his wife, St Stephen's, c. 1370. (© StSteph, DB)

16

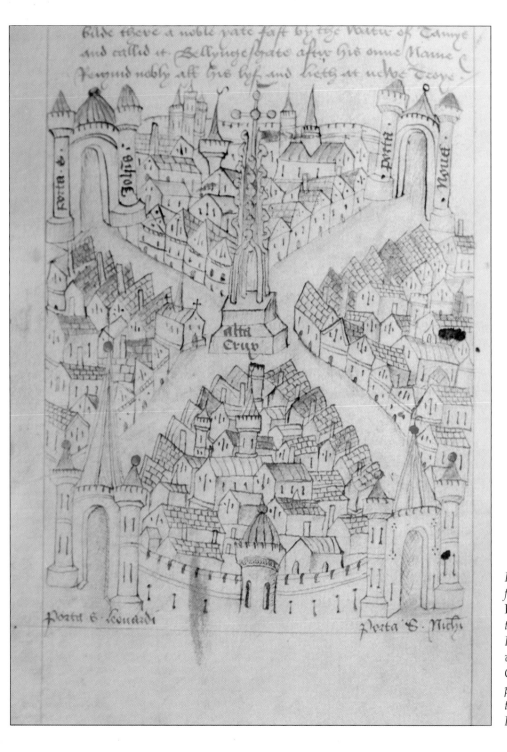

Ricart's Plan of Bristol, c. 1479, from the Maire of Bristowe is Kalendar: *the earliest-known town plan in Britain. It shows Bristol's four main thoroughfares with the High Cross at the centre. Clockwise from top right, the four principal gates into the walled town are: Newgate, St Nicholas, St Leonard and St John. (© BRO)*

Illustration (believed to be by Ricart, the town clerk) of the city's annual mayor-making ceremony, from the Maire of Bristowe is Kalendar. In typical medieval fashion, the more important an individual the bigger he is depicted. At the top the incoming mayor places his hand on the bible held by the outgoing mayor. Below, the town clerk (Ricart himself) reads out the oaths from his Kalendar. Facing him is the sword-bearer. Eight mace-bearers surround the dais and on the right are the councillors. The third group, at the very bottom, are burgesses or townsfolk who were allowed to witness the ceremony (some of them seem rather inattentive!). The ceremony took place on Michaelmas Day (29 September), in the chapel of St George attached to the Guildhall on Broad Street. (© BRO)

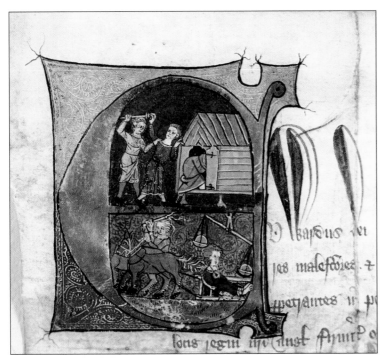

Illuminated initial letter, 1347 Bakers' Charter, showing (above) a lock-up for people found wandering the streets after dark without good reason, and (below) a baker found guilty of selling underweight or poor-quality bread being dragged through the streets with a loaf tied around his neck. (© BRO)

Initial letter, 1373 County Charter, depicting Edward III with the royal arms and the arms of Bristol. (© BRO)

William the Conqueror and William Rufus (grasping the arrow that killed him), both shown in fifteenth-century dress. Two of the vignettes of English kings from the Maire of Bristowe is Kalendar. *(© BRO)*

earth or stale urine (possibly collected from taverns or from receptacles in the street: the ammonia had a scouring effect). Next, the cloth was stretched, or tentered, on racks (hence the expression 'to be on tenter hooks'). Dyeing was usually carried out at this stage, after the woollen yarn had been woven: only rarely was an article 'dyed in the wool'. The most widely used dyestuff was woad, imported in vast quantities from Gascony, but the most highly prized was 'grain' or granum, from Spain or Portugal, used to produce the brilliant scarlet Broadmead cloth from which were made the gowns of mayors and councillors (had Robin Hood and his men really worn Lincoln 'grain' they would have stood out rather inconveniently in the greenwood!). The best cloth then had its nap raised with teazels, and then the nap was trimmed with shears.

Traditionally, fulling had been performed by pounding the cloth by hand or by treading it, rather like grapes, but by the end of the fourteenth century a technological revolution had swept the fulling industry. Water-powered fulling mills were springing up by fast-flowing streams throughout the countryside. The inevitable result was unemployment for many fullers, or tuckers as they were known in Bristol. The burgeoning rural fulling mills were acting like magnets, drawing away from the towns the livelihoods not only of the tuckers, but also of those involved in all stages of clothmaking. A new class of capitalist entrepreneurs, the clothiers, had emerged. Clothiers produced cloth for the London export market on the basis of rural 'cottage industry' grouped around the fulling mills, thereby sidestepping the restrictive practices and stringent quality regulations of the urban textile guilds. Most of the clothiers were Londoners, who could draw upon the resources of England's financial capital. One excep-

tion was Sir John Fastolf, a Yorkshire knight who invested some of his profits from a financially successful military career in the Hundred Years War in the cloth industry of Castle Combe in Wiltshire. Castle Combe supplied Sir John's retinue with their red and white uniforms, and under the capable management of his steward, none other than William Worcestre, the village grew into a veritable medieval boom town: but Sir John Fastolf's gain was Bristol's loss.

From the mid-1300s Bristol guilds tried unsuccessfully to prevent their members from dealing with producers in the surrounding valleys, with the excuse that the rural cloth was sub-standard, but

Tailors' Court, one of the few remaining medieval houses in the city. (© CM)

they were battling against the inevitable, and an irreversible decline set in during the fifteenth century. In 1461, in an attempt to safeguard male weavers' livelihoods, the Weavers' Guild attempted to ban female weavers, guildsmens' wives only excepted. While Bristol was increasingly eclipsed as a cloth producer, it continued to be a major local centre of the cloth trade, with a weekly cloth market in Tucker Street. However, by the early sixteenth century much of the cloth was produced outside the town walls, and many of the buyers were the very London clothiers whose activities were rapidly bringing about the Bristol cloth industry's demise.

> Divers persons of Weavers' Craft ... occupy
> and hire their wives, daughters and maidens,

Before its destruction in 1940, Temple Church had a chapel devoted to St Catherine, the patron saint of the Weavers' Guild. These stained-glass images from the chapel windows portray the saint with the spiked wheel on which she was tortured before being beheaded, and a weaver praying for her intercession on his behalf. (© BRO)

some to weave in their own looms and some to hire them to work with other persons of the same craft, by the which many and divers of the King's liege people ... goeth vagrant and unoccupied, and may not have their labour to their living.

(*Little Red Book*, Ordinances of the
Weavers' Guild)

Bristol businesspeople did not only have outside competition and trade cycles to worry about. From 1348 a combination of plague (the Black Death) and famine had killed off between a third and a half of the population of England. This catastrophe had brought about a severe shortage of workers. Employers were now having to compete with each other in attracting scarce labour. In Bristol as elsewhere the authorities tried in vain to keep wages at their pre-1348 level with a series of ordinances. But ordinances could not buck the market, and the period from 1373 to 1542, by which time the population had at last risen sufficiently to begin to tip the balance once more in the employer's favour, could be described as the 'golden age of labour'.

And in case that the said labourers are rebellious or factious and of their malice will not work then the ... masters shall have power to ... bring them before the Mayor at the court of the Guildhall... to be there justified according to law and right.

(*Little Red Book*, Fullers' Ordinances, 1406)

The wives of the masters of the craft ... have given and promised to their servants privily certain courtesies and gifts over and above their covenant.

Servants of the ... craft have departed out of the service of their masters without leave or license ... disporting themselves in the streets for two or three days a week.

(*Little Red Book*, Cordwainers'
Ordinances, 1408)

In common with other towns, Bristol's crafts and trades were organised into guilds. These were not the medieval equivalent of trades unions, but were more like employers' associations or modern chambers of commerce combined with friendly societies. They regulated their particular trade, ensuring the maintenance both of quality standards and their members' privileges (which often meant restricting the right of outsiders to carry out their trade), and represented their interests to outside bodies such as Bristol Corporation. In addition they provided support for members' families in the event of death or sickness. They also had important religious functions, which are dealt with later on (see 'Priests and Pulpits'). By 1450 there were at least twenty craft guilds in Bristol.

No manner of man henceforth shall trim or shave any person ... within ... Bristol unless he be a burgess and master of the ... craft [of barbers], their servants and apprentices ... provided always that it shall be lawful to every household servant of every burgess ... to shave and trim his master, his sons, daughters and household servants.

(*Little Red Book*, Barbers' Ordinances 1418)

If any one shall presume to sell flour adulterated with oats or in any way falsely compounded, for the first occasion let him be

severely fined, if convicted a second time let him lose all his flour, and a third time let him undergo the punishment of the pillory; for the fourth time let him abjure the town.
(*Little Red Book*, 14th-century Ordinances)

That no taverner of wine or ale keep any guests sitting in their taverns after the hour of curfew has rung under the penalty of 2 *s*., but shall immediately close his doors.
(*Little Red Book*, 14th-century Proclamations)

One very particular variety of trade guild was the association of overseas merchants, that is, those merchants who traded in bulk with foreign ports. In 1467 and again in 1500 Bristol's leading overseas merchants came together in an attempt to form their own guild. On both occasions the aim was to protect their interests, particularly in the Iberian trade, by excluding those who were not specialist overseas traders and by providing a supportive framework for those who were. Both attempts failed, and it was not until 1552, with the foundation of the Society of Merchant Venturers, that a permanent merchants' guild was successfully established in Bristol.

CROWNS AND CHARTERS

Our account of Cabot's Bristol begins in 1373 with the granting of two royal charters. Such documents, written in Latin and stuffed with legal jargon, might seem far removed from the day-to-day concerns of anyone except lawyers and bureaucrats, but these charters, and another granted in 1499, would touch the lives of generations of Bristolians. They also remind us that Bristol, like any community in medieval England, was not an island: just as its economy depended on constant commerce with those beyond its walls, so was the course of its politics determined by events on a national or even international stage.

Before 1373 Bristol was already a borough, that is, a community with its own legal identity whose inhabitants enjoyed freedom from the payment of many tolls and who could buy and sell land free of most feudal restrictions; in this it was no different from many other towns throughout England. But in that year, two charters granted by King Edward III made Bristol unique among provincial towns by giving it the status of a county: in 1373 only London enjoyed such privileges. Henceforth, in addition to the existing mayor and common council, common to English boroughs, Bristol was to have its own sheriff and its own county courts; it was also to have the right to elect members of parliament with the same status as knights of the shire, as opposed to the less prestigious parliamentary burgesses who represented other provincial towns. After 1446 Bristol followed the shires in that these MPs were to be elected by males with freehold property worth at least two pounds per year. The boundaries of the new county and town of Bristol included the suburbs of Redcliffe and Temple Fee, whose past relationships with Bristol had been ambiguous and fraught with tension, and extended into the middle of the Bristol Channel as far as Steep Holm and Flat Holm. However, the Castle, as a royal possession, was not

This illustration, taken from the Maire of Bristowe is Kalendar, *shows the first sheriff of Bristol appointed after the creation of the County in 1373. He is flanked by two officers armed with mace and axe. (© BRO)*

21

The other side of the seal matrix illustrated on p. 12 represents the stone keep of Bristol Castle. Notice the man blowing a trumpet from the ramparts! (© BRO)

included within the county boundaries, and so remained an island of Gloucestershire within the county of Bristol. This new status is striking testimony to Bristol's economic importance in the later fourteenth century, but to discover why these charters were granted at that precise moment we need to consider events far away from the west of England.

By the early 1370s England had been fighting France for over thirty years, and the war was not going well for the ageing king. Edward desperately needed money for the war effort, and Bristol, one of the wealthiest towns in the realm, was not a temptation he could afford to resist. In 1372 he claimed some of the profits of Bristol's borough courts and

administration as his own; probably more important than the loss of revenue to the Corporation was the attack this represented on Bristol's independence, since the right to these dues was a jealously guarded symbol of the town's exercise of self-government. The mayor and councillors came to terms with the king: if he would guarantee their independence and establish Bristol as England's second urban county, they would pay him the considerable sum of £400; he agreed, and so the town and county of Bristol was born.

County status brought undoubted benefits to the people of Bristol. Previously, Bristol north of the Avon had been part of Gloucestershire, while Redcliffe and Temple Fee were in Somerset, with the result that Bristolians with business at county courts had to travel either to Gloucester or to Ilchester or Taunton, depending on which side of the river they lived; after 1373 such journeys were unnecessary. Bristol now had its own panoply of courts, including the mayor's court, which was competent to deal with all civil pleas and handled writs from the king; the tolzey court, whose name derived from 'toll house', and which had particular jurisdiction over commercial matters; the piepowder court, an offshoot of the tolzey which sat when fairs were held to dispense immediate justice in cases involving traders from outside Bristol (its name derives from the Old French *pieds poudrés*, 'dusty feet', in other words those countryfolk who had walked to the Bristol fairs); and the staple court, which dealt mainly with disputes over commercial credit. The range of courts dealing with commercial matters is very noticeable, and reflects Bristol's position as a major trading centre. However, the mayor's courts did not confine themselves to the regulation of commerce, and Bristolians lived in an intensely regulated world: at least on paper, for the number of times that certain ordinances had to be repeated suggests that their acceptance and enforcement was far from complete. Among many issues, Bristol's legislators were concerned with keeping the streets clean and free from obstruction, and there seems to have been a particular problem with straying livestock. A tariff of penalties was introduced for the owners of wandering animals, from a few pennies for a straying duck to six shillings for a pig; penalties increased for repeat offenders, and so to distinguish pigs with a record the first time the animal strayed its tail was cut, the second a nick was made on its head and for the third offence the pig was given to the prisoners in the town gaol for their dinner.

> That no one wander by night about the town after sound of curfew unless he carry a lighted candle under pain of imprisonment.
> If any priest being in the service of any burgess shall be publicly taken in fornication let him be removed immediately.
> That no one of whatsoever condition he shall be throw urine or stinking or fouled water in the streets out of window or door.
> That no one occupy the highways or lanes in the town or suburb of Bristol with dung, rubbish or timber.
> That no lepers hereafter stay in the town under pain of imprisonment.
>
> (*The Little Red Book*, Ordinances)

The people who benefited most from the 1373 charters were the elite of the town's burgesses. A burgess enjoyed the freedom of the borough; in other words, he – in medieval Bristol all burgesses were male – was able to buy and sell without the restrictions placed on lesser traders, and he had the right to

The Little Red Book of Bristol. *Begun in 1344, it contained numerous ordinances by which the authorities attempted to regulate the daily life of the town. (© BRO)*

participate in the town's government. The 1373 charters confirmed Bristol's government as an oligarchy (a small group of wealthy individuals): the number of councillors was reduced from 48 to 40, and they were to be chosen, 'with the consent of the community', from among the wealthier burgesses by the mayor and sheriff. These two officers were in turn drawn from among the councillors, the mayor by annual election, and the sheriff by the king's selection from a list of three candidates presented by the common council. Almost all of the councillors were substantial merchants, and the mayor was a figure of particular importance, surrounded by pomp and ceremony.

The next important stage in Bristol's constitutional development was a charter of 1499. This recognised the structure that had evolved since 1373 following the lead of London's government: an inner elite of five aldermen, one for each of Bristol's five wards (Trinity, St Mary-le-Port, All Saints, St Ewen and Redcliffe), who doubled as justices of the peace; one of the aldermen was to fill the office of recorder, a senior law officer who was also expected to represent Bristol's interests to crown and parliament. The number of sheriffs was increased from one to two. The main intention behind this charter was probably to improve the effectiveness of law enforcement within the town and county, but in so doing it tightened the grip of this self-selecting oligarchy of a mere 43 men on a complex community 10,000 strong. Whatever its faults, the constitution established between 1373 and 1499 was to remain largely unaltered until the Municipal Reform Act of 1835 brought a modicum of democracy into urban politics.

While there is no evidence of any deep-rooted objections to the principle of oligarchy, there was criticism of individual mayors and councillors. In 1422 the common council passed an ordinance by which fines could be imposed on anyone villifying the mayor, councillors or their officials. The following three examples indicate the sort of behaviour the 1422 ordinance was intended to curtail.

On the afternoon of Friday 12 March 1479 Mayor William Spencer and Sheriff John Skrevyn were hearing cases in the Mayor's Court on Corn Street. Thomas Norton esquire, one of the royal customs officers, or customers, for Bristol, strode into court,

read out an accusation of treason against the mayor, and threw down his gauntlet as a challenge. Such an act was unheard of. Naturally, the mayor denied the charge, but Norton appealed to the sheriff to see that justice be done. The mayor decided that he had to clear his name and so the next day he gave up his office and had the sheriff convey him to the prison in Newgate until the king had decided his guilt or innocence. Deputies from the common council and Norton himself appeared before King Edward IV to put their separate cases. The common council deputies praised Mayor Spencer's exemplary character, and painted a damning picture of Norton. They claimed that Norton had robbed and threatened members of his own family, and now spent his nights in taverns and his mornings in bed, and played tennis and other immoral sports when he should have been in church. More particularly, they alleged that he had illegally retained in his service a gang of thugs, for which offence the mayor had prosecuted him. Defending himself against this charge, Norton had claimed that he was only retaining these men to help him search for contraband. He also claimed that Mayor Spencer was among the smugglers, and that the charge of illegal retaining was prompted by the mayor's anger at Norton's refusal of a barrel of wine as a bribe to turn a blind eye to his shipments of untaxed cloth. For their part, the deputies alleged that it was in revenge for the prosecution for retaining that Norton had brought the wholly baseless charge of treason against the mayor. According to the record in the town's official archives, when Norton was required to substantiate his charge of treason he was unable to lay any evidence before the king, and the case was dismissed. Mayor Spencer was released from Newgate, amid great rejoicing, and resumed his office. Norton's eventual fate is unknown.

John Wilkyns [one of Norton's associates] ... said by his oath that he ... called the mayor Ape's Face and cursed him for that he had committed him to gaol.

(*The Great Red Book*)

In 1518 there was further dissention, this time within the ruling elite. Sheriff William Dale brought a case before the royal court of Star Chamber at Westminster, in which he alleged that the mayor and common council forced younger merchants to accept the office of sheriff and then imposed enormous and unreasonable expenses on them. With the exaggeration typical of the time Dale went on to claim that this brought about not only the sheriffs' ruin, but also led to the desolation of about 700 households! Star Chamber found against Dale, and ruled that much of his expenditure was the result of his own personal extravagance, while the £38 3*s*. 6*d*. in genuine expenses that the sheriff had to meet from his own purse was a reasonable price to pay for such an honourable position. This case had cost the common council dear in money and time, and had soured relations between mayor and sheriff: the official record notes with undisguised glee how after the judgement Dale was forced to humble himself before the common council, and a special committee was formed to arrange appropriate punishments for Dale and his supporters.

William Dale ... confederated with divers other ill-disposed persons of the town to infringe and break the ancient and laudable usages, customs and orders of the town to the great unquieting, trouble and vexation of the town and to the perilous example of other like offenders ....
William Dale came into the ... Common Council

house ... and then and there in right obedient manner with watery tears submitted himself.

(*The Great White Book*)

The third example concerns Bristol's Irish population. Bristol's links with Ireland went back at least to the Norman conquest of the island, but in the fifteenth century large parts of Ireland were in open rebellion against English rule, and the town's substantial Irish population became the object of the mayor and common council's suspicion. In 1439 ordinances prohibited Irishmen from holding office in the common council and in some of the guilds, and Irish 'rebels' were not to be employed as servants. In the mid-1450s a burgess of Irish extraction, Henry May, alleged in the royal Chancery Court at Westminster that the mayor had been persecuting him and his associates, and had removed their rights as burgesses because of their Irish birth. The court ordered that May and his fellows should be reinstated as burgesses, but the mayor insisted that they should pay handsomely for this privilege. According to the triumphalist note in the Corporation records, the Irish burgesses were indeed forced to buy back their rights in a most humiliating fashion.

[Henry May and his fellows] with the blood of their purses, and with weeping eyes, kneeling on their knees, besought the mayor and his brethren of their grace.

(*The Maire of Bristowe is Kalendar*)

As well as campaigning in Ireland and France, from 1399 the English were also fighting amongst themselves. In that year Richard II was deposed by Henry Bolingbroke, who ascended the throne as Henry IV, first of the Lancastrian kings. Bristol was conspicuously loyal to Bolingbroke. During the usurpation Bristol willingly surrendered itself to Henry and three of King Richard's hated favourites, Scrope, Bushy and Green, were besieged in the Castle. They gave up after four days and after a peremptory trial were beheaded at the High Cross. In a decidedly unsubtle gesture Henry sent their heads in a basket to London, with a note asking which side the Londoners were on! A few months later another of Richard's supporters, Thomas Despencer, earl of Gloucester, was also beheaded at the High Cross, this time by a lynch mob. Henry IV made a gift of Despencer's furred gown to the leader of the mob. Henry IV and his son, the future Henry V, had to face opposition from a different quarter when Owain Glyndwr led a Welsh rebellion which threatened to oust English rule. Bristol was very well sited to play a key role in the English war effort, and supplied men and ships in great quantities, and manufactured cannon for the king's army.

Henry VI, the third and final Lancastrian king, was incompetent and mentally unstable, and during the 1450s his hold on power grew ever weaker. The chief critic of Henry's government was Richard duke of York, who had been appointed lieutenant of Ireland in order to remove him from English politics. In the summer of 1450, with popular rebellion sweeping across the southern counties of England, fears that Richard of York would invade combined with those of French raids or even invasion. Bristol was an obvious target for both York and the French, and so great efforts were made to repair its walls and to increase its stock of artillery.

> [It] was ordained and decreed that £40 of common money should be had and delivered … and therewith [should be purchased] certain guns and other stuff necessary for defence of the said town … Item, a dozen brazen guns to be made shooting pellets as great as a Paris ball or less and every gun with 4 chambers
> (*The Great Red Book*, 1450)

These measures may have been taken to repel an attack by Richard of York, but the duke held property at King's Barton on the outskirts of Bristol and had well-placed friends in town, and the townsfolk seem to have become more sympathetic towards him as Henry VI's Lancastrian regime stumbled through the 1450s. In 1451 Thomas Young, one of York's attorneys and a Bristol MP, was imprisoned in the Tower of London for raising in parliament the question of his master's claim to the throne. At this stage, Young's enthusiasm for the 'Yorkist' cause was not shared by the mayor and common council: the following year they received a letter from the duke requesting their support in an armed demonstration against the king, which they passed straight to the government. However, there was sufficent popular opposition to Henry VI to provoke a special judicial commission of enquiry to investigate stories of rebellious activity in and around Bristol, and the town had to buy a general pardon for the past offences of its inhabitants, while in 1453 there was a rumour that a group of Bristol merchants had been casting spells to bring about the king's mental collapse. But by the late 1450s, as the battle lines of the 'Wars of the Roses' began to be drawn, even the mayor was prepared to declare openly for the Yorkist rebels: gunpowder sent by the king to Bristol for safe keeping was requisitioned by the mayor, William Canynges, and, under instructions from Richard of York was used to prepare Bristol Castle against a possible Lancastrian attack.

Richard of York was killed in battle in 1460, but the following year his son defeated the Lancastrians, with the aid of the powerful Richard earl of Warwick, known as 'the Kingmaker', and took the throne as King Edward IV. The Bristol elite seem to have transferred their loyalties from father to son without too much hesitation. Twice in the first year of Edward's reign the mayor and common council provided ships at their own expense for campaigns against Lancastrian die-hards in Wales.

In September 1461 Edward IV visited Bristol, where he was 'full honorably received in as worshipful wise as ever there was'. The king was met at Temple Gate by an actor playing William the Conqueror, and a giant handed him the town's keys; the next pageant was acted out at Temple Cross, where St George slew the Dragon and angels sang in celebration. The play-acting over, Edward presided over some real blood-letting. A Devonshire Lancastrian, Sir Baldwin Fulford, had vowed either to destroy the earl of Warwick or lose his head. He kept the second part of his oath, and with two Bristol associates was executed, according to tradition at the High Cross while Edward and his courtiers looked on from the east window of St Ewen's church. As a reward for their good service, in 1462 the king granted financial privileges to the people of Bristol. The mayor, Philip Mead, was reported to have 'sped full well with the king's good grace' during his audience with Edward IV on this occasion.

> Welcome Edward, our son of high degree,
> Many years hast thou been out of this land,
> I am your forefather, William of Normandy,
> To see thy welfare here through God's hand
> ('William the Conqueror's' speech to
> Edward IV, 1461)

This honeymoon period did not last long. Lancastrian loyalties were certainly not dead. In 1463 a special judicial commission investigated insurrections in the Bristol region. But the real threat to Edward's power was to come from a wholly unexpected quarter. By 1469 Warwick the Kingmaker was feeling let down by the man he had helped to make king. Warwick made an extraordinary alliance with the king's own brother, George, duke of Clarence, and his former bitter enemy, the Lancastrian queen Margaret of Anjou, in order to put her husband, Henry VI, back on the throne. By now Henry was totally incapable of ruling even himself, and this was really a plan to allow Warwick, Margaret and Clarence to rule through this lamentable puppet king.

Forced to choose between Edward and the Warwick party, many Bristolians plumped for the latter. The duke of Clarence held substantial West Country estates, and it may be that his role as local patron was the crucial factor deciding Bristol loyalties. After the defeat of Edward's great ally, William Herbert, earl of Pembroke, at Edgecote near Banbury in 1469, his brother, Sir Thomas Herbert, was captured and brought to Bristol, where he was executed. The next year Warwick and Clarence, with the assistance of West Countrymen, succeeded in ousting Edward and put Henry VI back on the Throne. Gloucestershire was not immune to the chaos that briefly engulfed the realm in 1470: at Nibley Green, a few miles north of Bristol, the private armies of Lord Berkeley and Viscount Lisle met in pitched battle, the culmination of years of squabbling over an inheritance. Among the Berkeley retinue was a group of Bristolians, led by Philip Mede, a prominent Bristol merchant related to the Berkeleys by marriage.

The tomb of Philip Mede (d. 1471) and his wife in St Mary Redcliffe. This beautifully sculpted tomb, with its angels struggling to lift Philip's head, is very similar to one dedicated to Richard Choke in Long Ashton church, and is almost certainly by the same craftsman. (© StMR, DB)

But Edward IV returned from exile in 1471 with an army of fellow exiles and foreign mercenaries, and by now he had managed to win back the loyalty of his spectacularly shifty brother Clarence. After defeating and killing Warwick at Barnet, Edward marched towards the South West to give battle to Margaret of Anjou. Margaret's army had landed at Weymouth, and marching north reached Bristol at the end of April. Here they found a large number of well-wishers, and were able to use the royal mint in Bristol Castle to coin money to pay for wages and further supplies. But all this was to no avail. Three days after leaving Bristol Margaret was defeated at Tewkesbury. Among those killed was Bristol's recorder, and other Bristol men had joined Margaret's army. The Lancastrian cause now seemed irredeemably lost.

[Margaret's army] went to Bristol, a good and strong walled town, where they were greatly refreshed and relieved by such as were the king's rebels in that town, with money, men, and artillery.

(*The Arrival of Edward IV*)

Secure once again on his throne, Edward did not forget the help Bristol had given to his enemies. The king replaced Bristol's sheriff, and while he granted a general pardon to Bristol (at the urging of Clarence), eight Bristolians exempted from the pardon were ordered to be arrested and to have their property confiscated.

And albeit that the inhabitants of our town of Bristol have not been of such demeaning of late in their duty and alleagance as they ought to have been towards us, yet forasmuch as our dearest brother the duke of Clarence has specially instanced us to be gracious lord unto the town and to you, notwithstanding the offences committed by the generality of the town, but only by certain persons of the same, we inclined at his special request to ... [punish] the principal stirrers of rebellion against us and not the generality

(*The Little Red Book*, Edward IV's proclamation, 1471)

Henceforth Bristol had to tread carefully in its relations with the king. Edward visited Bristol in 1475 to raise forced 'loans' from the more substantial citizenry to help pay for a projected invasion of France, and he raised an enormous sum, for none of those asked seems to have thought it wise to refuse him! Despite their victory in 1471 the Yorkists still feared Lancastrian claimants, most notably the exiled Henry Tudor, earl of Richmond. Accusations of treason were potent weapons, but could easily backfire. In 1479 Roger Markes of Bristol accused Robert Strange, late mayor, of coining money and sending it to the earl of Richmond; but Strange was cleared of this charge, and it was Markes who suffered the traitor's death he had wished on his enemy.

In 1485 Henry Tudor defeated Edward's younger brother and successor, Richard III, and took the throne as Henry VII. The following year he made his first visit to Bristol. The town gave him a grand reception. The royal party was met three miles out of Bristol by the mayor, sheriffs, bailiffs and other burgesses, who accompanied Henry to Lafford's Gate (Lawford's Gate at the end of Old Market), where he was greeted by a procession of the town's four orders of friars. At Newgate Henry came face to face with another 'king': Brennius, the Trojan prince who, it was then believed, had founded Bristol with his brother Bellinus. The actor playing this part greeted Henry as his 'most dear cousin' and went on to tell how from the prosperity in which Brennius had left it, the town had declined as a result of the recent slump in overseas trade and clothmaking. Other delights awaited the king, such as an elephant – presumably artificial – with a castle on its back, in the

Statues of Brennius and Bellinus are set in niches on either side of St John's Gate, the only surviving medieval entrance into the town. They probably replaced pre-Reformation effigies of saints. (© CM)

highest tower of which was a mechanical representation of the resurrection of Christ, but the real point of the lavish spectacle had been made by King Brennius: Bristol was a loyal, ancient and great town, but right now it needed help. The message was not lost on the king. He summoned the mayor, the sheriff, and the leading burgesses, and listened as they explained that Bristol had suffered a great loss of ships in the previous five years. He promised help, but it is unclear what, if anything, was forthcoming.

I am right glad, ye be welcome to this land,
Namely to this town, which I Brennius king,
Once builded with her walls old,
And called it Bristow in the beginning
('Brennius's' speech to Henry VII, 1486)

Whatever help Henry may have given was clawed back, probably with advantages, four years later. In 1490, on his second visit, he exacted the enormous sum of £500 in unofficial tax (called a 'benevolence'). Bristol supposedly paid dearly because the sumptuous appearance of the burgesses' wives convinced Henry that their husbands' earlier plea of poverty had been, to say the least, over-imaginative. Henry's harsh taxation provoked a major rebellion in 1497: an army of Cornishmen marched on London, and en route they demanded that Bristol provide them with shelter and support. But the burgesses resisted them, wisely balancing the unpleasant consequences of supporting a failed rebellion against the recent memory of empty purses.

The mayor mustered and made ready to withstand the rebels, and garnished the town walls with men harnessed and with guns and brought ships and boats about the marsh, garnished with men, artillery and guns
(*The Maire of Bristowe is Kalendar*)

The remainder of Henry VII's reign was far less eventful, and for twenty years or so after the accession of his son Henry VIII in 1509 Bristol was able to get on with the business of making money in relative peace. What overturned this tranquil state of affairs, and what brings our own account to an end, was the Reformation, but this will have to wait for another chapter ('Priests and Pulpits').

PAUPERS AND MERCHANT PRINCES

In Bristol, as elsewhere in medieval England, differences between rich and poor were stark. The wealthy burgesses – veritable 'merchant princes' – preferred to live close to their warehouses, shops and workshops, which meant that they lived cheek by jowl with the poor: smart residential suburbs like Hotwells, Clifton and Redland were two hundred years in the future. The contrasts would have been all the more apparent because of the very public and visual nature of medieval culture and society. With their grand houses, luxurious clothes and posses of servants, the rich flaunted their wealth; the poor, in hope of charity, flaunted their poverty. Even in posterity the gulf between the haves and have-nots remains, since the rich have bequeathed to us a wealth of evidence from which we can reconstruct their lives, while the poor could leave us almost nothing. What evidence we do have of the lives of the humble majority of Bristol's population was produced by their superiors: through their eyes, the poor appear to us as the objects of charity, condescension, suspicion, fear, or barely concealed disgust. The crucial social division in Bristol lay between the burgesses, those who enjoyed the freedom of full citizenship, and the rest.

The freedom enjoyed by a burgess, as well as giving him the right to participate in the political life of the town, also brought important economic privileges, amounting to the right to trade without

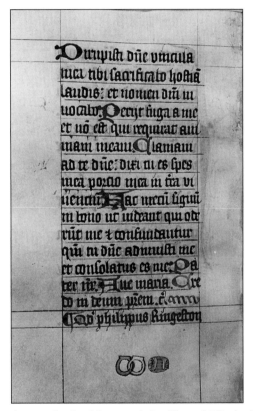

Page from a book of hours of the Blessed Virgin Mary made for Philip Ringeston, a Bristol merchant, in 1479. A cartoon at the bottom shows two rings and a tun (a type of barrel), as a pun on his surname. (© CRL)

restrictions and without paying tolls. Non-freemen had no political voice and laboured under a number of economic disabilities, which in effect meant that they could only trade on the fringes of Bristol's economy, and were largely condemned to work in the workshops and houses of the burgesses, or else take their chances on the streets. Significantly, they were known as 'strangers', even if Bristol born and bred. For them, Bristol was a home to which they did not fully belong.

The means of entry into the male elite of burgesses in Bristol were similar to those in most other English towns. The simplest way was for the son of a burgess to inherit his father's freedom on coming of age. For men not born to the freedom, it could be bought (this was known as redemption), or entrance could be attained through apprenticeship to a burgess or to his widow, or by marriage to the daughter or widow of a burgess.

Medieval common law imposed a variety of restrictions on the extent to which property-holders could dispose of their possessions, partly in order to safeguard the position of heirs. In Bristol many aspects of common law did not apply. Here, the borough law gave property-owners complete freedom to dispose of land and houses as they wished, but at their death one third of their chattels (moveable property such as money, clothes, furniture, and merchandise) normally had to go to their children and, in the case of husbands, one-third to their wives; the remaining third would pay for funeral expenses and prayers. In a trading community like Bristol, a far greater proportion of property was held in the form of chattels than would have been the case with the country gentry and nobility, the bulk of whose income was usually derived from land, but the borough law did mean that

A house on Temple St, from a plan book made in 1817 which illustrates properties belonging to the estate of the parish of St Thomas the Martyr. Although the building shows evidence of later reconstruction, its dimensions suggest that it was of Tudor or later medieval construction. (© StThom, DB)

while the eldest son of a burgess would inherit his freedom and some of his goods, he could not count on taking over his father's house or lands. This would have given Bristol fathers enormous power over their children: a disobedient son could find

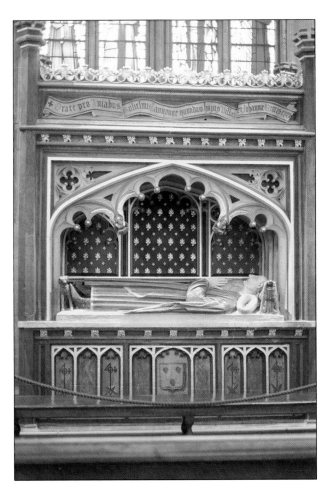

*Tomb of William Canynges (d. 1474)
and his wife Joan in St Mary Redcliffe.
(© StMR, DB)*

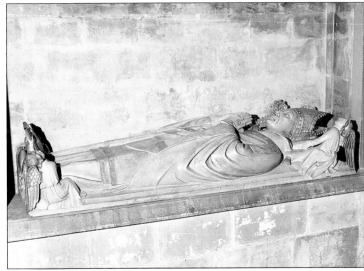

*Tomb of Abbot Newland, Bristol Cathedral. Newland was abbot of St
Augustine's Abbey at the time of Cabot's 1497 voyage. His nickname
was 'Nailheart', from his personal badge of a heart and the three nails
of Christ's passion (shown on a shield at his feet). (© DB)*

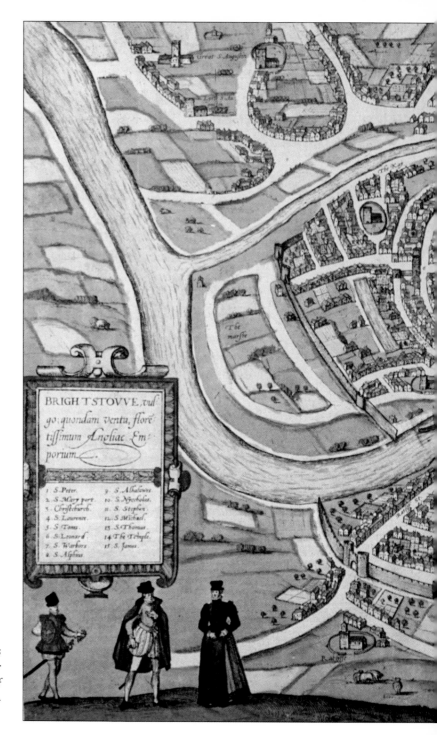

Hoefnagle's plan of Bristol, 1581. Although it was produced nearly forty years after the end of our period, this early, somewhat stylised view of Bristol is included here because it gives an evocative impression of the Tudor city. (© CM)

The east end of Bristol Cathedral. This is the medieval section of the cathedral, from the central tower eastwards, which formed part of the church of the Abbey of St Augustine, largely rebuilt in the later Middle Ages. (© CM)

The south aisle of Bristol Cathedral. The interior displays the high-quality, innovative workmanship of the later medieval rebuilding. (© DB) himself literally without a roof over his head after his father's death.

Bristol's burgesses imposed strict controls over admittance to their charmed circle. Redemptioners had to pay a £10 entrance fee. This was a great deal of money: a country gentleman could maintain himself and his household adequately on an annual income of £10. In addition, redemptioners needed two burgess sponsors, and after the early fifteenth century they could only be admitted with the assent of the mayor, sheriff and common council.

Apprenticeship was a more usual means of entry. In the first half of the sixteenth century, most Bristol apprentices began their training around the age of fifteen, after perhaps no more than one year's formal schooling, ending their apprenticeships after seven years. The apprentice joined the master's household, and there learned not only the skills of the craft, but also the various social skills and etiquette that would be necessary in respectable adult society. Over three-quarters of early sixteenth-century apprentices came from outside Bristol, with significant numbers from Wales and Ireland, and of the Bristolians the vast majority were apprenticed outside their parents' households. So apprenticeship served to pump new blood into Bristol society. But it was not an automatic ticket to prosperity. Apprentices could only be admitted to the freedom if their masters or other men of repute vouched for their suitability, and only one-third of sixteenth-century apprentices actually became burgesses. The rest probably either maintained a precarious existence in the town or else took advantage of the expanding opportunities in rural trade and industry to practise their crafts outside Bristol.

The vast majority of apprentices were boys, but there was a tiny number of girls. Of these, most were apprenticed to women, to be trained in the arts of needlework and housekeeping. In other words, they were to be given the skills necessary to attract first, employment as domestic servants and then, with luck, husbands.

> Here at Bristol dwelleth one,
> Is held a right just, true man,
> As I hear now tell;
> His apprentice will I be seven years
> His science truly for to learn,
> And with him will I dwell
> (John Lydgate, 'The Childe of Bristow',
> 15th century)

Nearly all Bristolians of the burgess class married, and most chose their partners from among their peers. Mayor Philip Mede, whose daughter married Sir Maurice Berkeley, Lord of Beverston, of the Berkeleys of Berkeley Castle, was an exception, and few burgesses sought marriages with the land-holding gentry or nobility. Marriage then, was no match for apprenticeship when it came to revitalising the Bristol gene pool.

That Bristol's population did need to be replenished from outside is suggested by mortality rates among the merchants. The average age at death was 52 (actually a couple of years more than in London, perhaps because Bristol's system of fresh water conduits gave it a relatively healthier environment). Not surprisingly, about one-fifth of merchants married more than once. Infant mortality was particularly high, and despite fairly frequent pregnancies most families had only two children surviving at their father's death. The result was that few burgess families lasted more than three generations. This, in turn, meant that political dynasties and massive a smaller sum than the redemptioner's fee and attain lesser trading privileges as portwomen or portmen. The 'port' element in these terms has nothing to do with the usual modern sense of port (as in 'the port of Bristol'), but derives from an old word meaning market or trade (hence, St Mary-le-Port, at whose gates a market was held in the Middle Ages). Most portwomen and men probably sold food, often coming into Bristol from the surrounding countryside to do so. The legal status of these small retailers declined markedly during the fifteenth century. By an ordinance of 1454–5 traders could be admitted to the rank of portman or woman on payment of an annual fee of 3s. 4d., but they were only allowed to sell bread and ale in the town's markets. Sixteen years later even this limited privilege was revoked, and henceforth they could do no more than hawk bread and ale around the streets, with the exception of five country bakers who were allowed stalls in Bristol to supplement the town's own bread ovens.

> All women that sell fish should stand upon the
> Back and in no other places, upon pain of 40d.
> (*The Great Red Book*)

Brewing ale and selling both this and bread were traditionally female occupations (women are also found selling fish, wool and thread), and it is likely that portwomen far outnumbered portmen. For this reason, attempts by the male burgesses to restrict the activities of these lesser traders could have been part of a broader assault on women's economic position. We have already seen evidence of this in the weaving industry, and there was probably a common motive: in increasingly difficult trading conditions, the men who controlled the trades were trying to preserve their own jobs at the expense of women.

St John's Conduit pump was moved to Nelson Street in 1827. Bristol's network of conduits supplying fresh water was unusually complete by medieval standards. (© CM)

agglomerations of property, both built up over generations, were not a usual feature of Bristol society: the Canynges dynasty, which provided a mayor of Bristol in each of three generations, provides a rare exception. Needless to say, among the lower orders this picture would have been even bleaker. Like other medieval towns, Bristol could not have sustained itself without a constant influx of would-be Dick Whittingtons from the countryside, which was healthier than the town, but traditionally less promising for the ambitious fortune-hunter.

Those unable to inherit, marry, train or buy their way into the full freedom of burgess status could pay

This 1820 drawing by H. O'Neill shows the St John's Conduit pump in its original location, in a stone conduit house on the inner side of St John's Gate. (© CRL)

Bristol's piped water was very costly, and the width of water pipes carefully controlled. This document granted the right to tap water from the main pipe through a subsidiary pipe called a 'feather'. The feather's spine is still attached! (© BRO)

Quite apart from being the wrong answer to the problem of unemployment, these restrictive ordinances wilfully ignored the crucial role played by craftsmen's wives in the household economy. Not only did these women supply valuable assistance to their husbands, they also owed it to their children, servants and apprentices to involve themselves in the craft so that in the event of their husbands' death

or incapacity they would be able to take over the business. Indeed, widows were expected to carry on their late husband's trade for at least as long as it took to find new masters for their apprentices and servants.

This expectation also applied to merchants' wives. An outstanding – and therefore atypical – example of an active merchant widow is provided by Alice

36

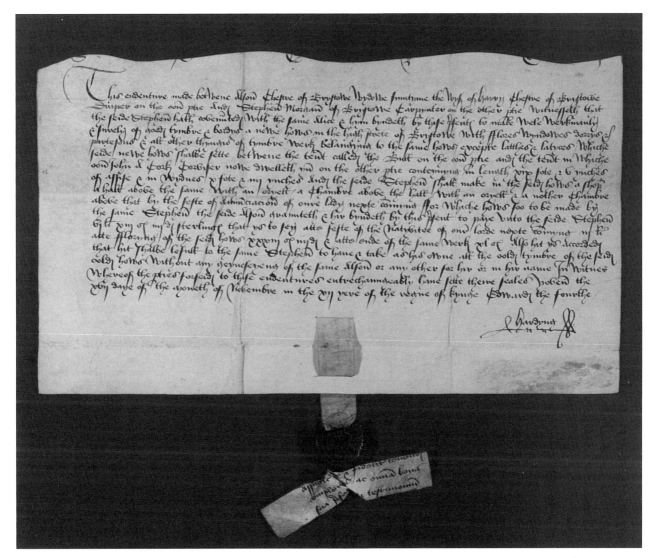

Alice Chestre, a rich widow who traded as a draper in her own right, signed this agreement with Stephen Morgan, carpenter, to build her a new house 'of good timber and boards' in High Street in 1472. (© BRO)

An early nineteenth-century drawing by H. O'Neill, showing Alice Chestre's house, No. 31 High Street (centre). By this time its façade had been altered, but the dimensions of the medieval house are still recognisable. (© CRL)

Chestre. From 1473 (three years after her husband's death) until her own demise in 1485 she appears in the Bristol customs accounts trading regularly in cloth, wine and other commodities with Ireland, Spain and Portugal, often in her own ships. As an active merchant, she appreciated the practical difficulties of handling cargoes, and in 1475 provided the £41 required to build the first crane on Welsh Back.

> For the common weal of this town and for the saving of merchants' goods, both of the town and of strangers, the tenth year before her death [Alice Chestre] let made at her own costs and charges a crane upon the Back by the Marsh Gate, where was never none before that time; the which cost her £41 and odd money, and of the crane a fair rent comes and rests yearly unto the Common Chamber of this town.
>
> (*All Saints' Church Book*)

Most merchant widows appear only to have traded long enough to honour their late husbands' contracts, but many Bristol merchants placed great trust in the commercial acumen of their female relatives, leaving them to run the business while they were away at sea. Unfortunately, much of our evidence for women running their absent menfolks' affairs comes from court cases, and so is the product of the rare occasions when such arrangements broke down. For example, in the early fifteenth century John Hethe, before embarking on a voyage, entrusted the sum of £200 and some property deeds to his unmarried sister. Hethe was shipwrecked and thrown into a foreign dungeon, and in the meantime his sister had been married and widowed. When he finally made it back home, the unfortunate Hethe

claimed that his sister, in whom he had once reposed 'great trust', had suffered a change of character, and now refused to return either the money or the deeds.

Others appointed their wives as the executors of their wills. The executor's role demanded considerable expertise and energy if the terms of the deceased's will were to be carried out and his estate properly administered. For husbands who left behind enormous debts, the task was fraught with danger, since the executor was liable to the deceased's creditors. One Bristol widow, named as executor by her heavily indebted husband, tried to evade this dubious honour by fleeing to London, taking with her only the clothes she stood up in: but to no avail, for her husband's creditors pursued her even there.

While a few women enjoyed relatively privileged economic and social positions, for many at the bottom of the heap opportunities were few. One option was prostitution. Town ordinances banned prostitutes from entering the town gates, and ordered them to wear striped hoods as a sign of their occupation. An ordinance of 1344 stated that if any prostitute were found to be living within the town walls the doors and windows of her dwelling were to be removed, thereby presumably making it difficult for her to carry on an occupation that demands a certain degree of privacy. The aim of these regulations was not to stamp out prostitution, which was regarded as a regrettable necessity, but to keep it out of the more select residential areas.

> No prostitute to come within the town but to abide still at the Bars.
> No prostitute to wander about the town without a striped hood.
>
> (*The Great Red Book*)

The church of St Mary Redcliffe contains a number of corbels like this one (dated c. 1320), supporting tiers of sculptures. Their expressions may suggest the sufferings of those at the bottom of society. (© StMR, DB)

The Black Death had meant that there were rather more opportunities for the survivors, but this does not mean that everyone was able to earn enough to support themselves or their families. Competition from rural and London clothiers and disruptions to commerce put pressure on Bristol's staple trades – more than once in the fifteenth century the town pleaded its poverty to royal tax collectors – and so there probably was significant unemployment in the town at various times. In addition to the seasonal or cyclical unemployed, those too old or sick to work provided an ever-present core of paupers. There was of course nothing like state welfare. But far from ignoring the needs of the poor, many wealthy Bristolians were actually rather keen to provide for their less fortunate neighbours.

There were basically two ways in which this could be done: either through doles – or alms – of money, food or clothes to the poor (what in later ages would be called 'outdoor relief'), or through almshouses and hospitals, where a certain number of poor could be given shelter (distant, and perhaps more humane, ancestors of the workhouse). Alms were probably given on a regular basis by the wealthier burgesses, but it is through the bequests made in their wills that we know most about this form of relief.

The majority of burgess wills provide for doles to be given to the poor at the deceased's funeral, or as part of later memorial services. By his will of 1397 Reginald Taylor gave alms to the lame and blind who lived on the Bristol streets: an indication that almshouses were then unable to meet the demand for shelter. Taylor was not unusual in specifying the type of poor he wished to relieve. William Frome directed his largesse to the 'honest poor', who, having lost everything through bad luck, did not wish to beg, and Roger Levedon excluded vagrant beggars in favour of impoverished and bedridden householders. Clearly, the aim was to select only the 'deserving poor', which must sometimes have meant that those most in need could not benefit! Some bequests could be generous: Walter Derby left seventeen tenements to be sold to provide alms for the poor. Most bequests, however, were counted out in pennies, and represented but a tiny fraction of the burgesses' total wealth.

Other needs were sometimes remembered. As part of the annual memorial service for the wealthy merchants, Alice and Henry Chestre, 20*d.* worth of bread was to be given to the prisoners in Bristol's Newgate gaol, and 4*d.* worth to the lepers in St Mary Magdalene's Hospital at Brightbow. Hugh Wythiford left £1 to each of twenty poor virgins – that is, unmarried women – to provide them with dowries so that they could afford to marry; Thomas Spencer shared this concern, and left a quantity of woad to provide dowries for all the poor virgins in the parish of St Werburgh's.

The fifteenth century saw a number of new almshouse foundations. During his lifetime William Canynges founded an almshouse on Redcliffe Hill, and after his death his executor, William Spencer, fulfilled the provisions of his will by founding a second in Lewins Mead. Richard Forster founded an almshouse by Redcliffe Gate, and John Forster built one at the top of what is now Christmas Steps. By 1471 one burgess was able to leave donations to no fewer than nine Bristol almshouses.

Some of the craft guilds also provided for their less fortunate members, with, for example, alms-houses built by the Weavers and Tuckers Guilds. In 1445 Bristol mariners petitioned the mayor to found an almshouse to support twelve poor sailors, together with priests to pray for those 'passing and labouring on the sea'; this was established at St Bartholomew's Hospital as the Fraternity of St Clement. The entry requirements were strict: the almshouse was to be supported by tolls paid by mariners using the port of Bristol, and no poor mariner was to be accepted unless he had paid his dues for seven years, and he also had to give the Fraternity all of his personal goods, save clothes and bedding. On the other hand, living conditions at John Forster's almshouse seem to have been reasonably pleasant: each of the eight poor men and five poor women had their own room, each with its strip of garden, and next door was the chapel of the Three Kings of Cologne with its own priest to minister to their spiritual needs.

The Bristol elite's impressive achievements in the field of poor relief were not simply – or primarily – motivated by concern for the welfare of their fellow men and women. Their other, overriding, concern was for the welfare of their own souls. In return for the material benefits of their charity, these donors expected that the poor, the sick and the imprisoned would pay them back with the spiritual benefits of their prayers. To fully understand how this worked, we must now explore the religious world of later medieval Bristol.

PRIESTS AND PULPITS

Religion pervaded medieval life. Belief in the literal truth of the Bible was general, and while a tiny but growing minority of heretics questioned the Church's assumed monopoly of the truth about God few, if any, seem not to have believed in his existence. Acceptance of the religious orthodoxy meant a belief in Heaven, Hell, and a third place: Purgatory. Only the very bad went to Hell, but only the very good went straight to Heaven. For the great majority of humanity, Purgatory was the immediate destination after death. Here, their souls would be purged of sin, so that they could at last enter Heaven. But this purgation could last for thousands of years, and involve torments which, while supposedly unimaginable, were none-theless the subject of preachers' most lurid flights of the imagination. A soul's period of torment could be shortened or eased by good works carried out either by the individual while alive, or on his or her behalf after death. In addition, one could pray to the saints, those blessed souls who had gone straight to Heaven, in the hope that through their influence the pains of Purgatory – or indeed, the unpleasantness of this world – might be lessened. This is known as intercession. Another option was the purchase of an indulgence, which promised relief from the flames of Purgatory for a specified period. In theory, indulgences were a form of penance, and could only work if the purchasers sincerely repented of their sins, but many of the laity – and perhaps a good many clergy – adopted a rather mechanistic approach towards

Eagle lectern, St Stephen's. It originally stood in Cabot's parish church of St Nicholas, who was, fittingly enough, the patron saint of sailors. (© StSteph, DB)

indulgences, and saw them as a sort of spiritual fire insurance.

One variety of good works, charity, has already been discussed. The other kind was prayers. For the rich (who perhaps tended to need them more than most) sophisticated cycles of prayers were said at their funerals and at memorial services held first a month after their burial and then on its anniversary. About one third of Bristol burgesses went further, and established a trust fund, based usually on the rental income from property held by trustees, to finance prayers to be said in perpetuity; these foundations were known as chantries. A few of the really wealthy even had special chantry chapels built in which prayers for their souls could be said.

A popular alternative for those who could not afford their own chantry was the religious guild, or fraternity. This was an association formed to look after the spiritual needs of its members on a corporate basis. The organisation of religious fraternities paralleled that of the craft guilds, and indeed, these latter were often closely associated with particular religious fraternities. The mariners' fraternity of St Clement has already been mentioned, and St John the Baptist's based in St Ewen's Church provides a similar example of a craft-related fraternity, this one associated with the Tailors' Guild. There were at least eleven religious fraternities in Bristol. The most popular was that based in the chapel of the Assumption of the Virgin Mary on Bristol Bridge.

But perhaps the most famous Bristol fraternity is the Guild of Kalends, which met in a corner house next to All Saints' Church. The Guild already had a long history in Cabot's day, perhaps dating back to before the Norman Conquest. It took its name from the fact that its members met on the first day of the month (called the 'calends' in the Roman calendar

still used in the Middle Ages). Both clergy and laity were members, but the clergy had control of the Guild, and it was they who provided its prime service: the performance of mass and intercessions for both living and dead members. The Guild also provided a number of other benefits to its members, benefits that included looking after the old and the sick, settling disputes, and arranging funerals and

St Stephen's church, from an 1825 plan book of church property. The tower, built by the stonemason Benedict Crosse and largely paid for by Mayor John Shipward in the 1470s, has gone through a number of reconstructions since it was toppled by a storm in 1703. (© CM)

commemorations. In addition, the church hierarchy saw the Guild of Kalends as an important weapon in its battle against heresy: its priests regularly preached sermons, and within the Guild House was a library of religious books for use by the Bristol clergy to help their own preaching. So, in addition to being a prayer factory, social club, arbitration service, and an insurance and welfare society, the Guild was also an evangelising centre. The greater burgesses tended to shun fraternities, since they did not need to pool their resources with anyone for their spiritual needs, and many even had their own private chapels attached to their houses, well equipped and complete with their own chaplain.

William Worcestre noted that 'the height of the tower of [St Mary] Redcliffe is 300 feet, of which 100 feet have been cast down by lightening'. The present spire is Victorian. (© CM)

Fraternities and private chapels supplemented but did not replace parish churches as centres of devotion. Bristol had eighteen parish churches. By modern standards this seems an enormous number for a population of around 10,000, but Bristol was actually underprovided when compared to the number of parish churches in such comparable cities as York and Norwich.

The surviving evidence strongly suggests that at least the property-owning Bristolians regarded their parish church with real affection and devotion. Bequests to parish churches were frequent and generous: more generous, on average, than those to the poor. Money might be provided for the maintenance of the church fabric, or for new building: many Bristol churches were given new towers, porches and chapels, or even entirely rebuilt in this period. Alternatively, service books and other items necessary for religious ceremonies might be given. The more unusual bequests include Edward Dawes' gift of a quantity of woad to allow St Werburgh's to buy a new pair of organs, and John and Agnes Jenkins's gift to All Saints' of a coconut shell made into a gilt standing cup with cover, weighing 37 ounces: one wonders how this exotic fruit found its way to Bristol! Another gift to All Saints' came from William Wytteney, who gave a collection of service books bound in one volume. This stood at the foot of the image of St Christopher, until the volume was stolen. It was discovered, appropriately enough for a volume dedicated to the patron saint of travellers, at the shrine of St James at Santiago de Compostella in Spain and returned to Bristol, only to be stolen once again, seemingly never to be returned!

William Warens, chantry priest, gave to the church a breviary to be chained in the church to the ease of all manner priests to say their service when they have not their own books with them, and also paid for the chaining.

Alice [Chestre] has had made in carved work a tabernacle with a Trinity in the middle over the image of Jesus, and also at her own cost had it gilded full worshipfully, with a cloth hanging before to be drawn at certain times when it shall please the vicar and parishioners.

Julian Papnam gave a chalice of 24 ozs, and bishop Carpenter of Worcester has given 40 days of pardon to everyone hearing the mass said with the same chalice on principal feasts.

(*All Saints' Church Book*)

William Canynges, exceptional in his devotion as in his wealth, went beyond the prayers and good works with which his peers were satisfied. After his wife's death in 1466 he took holy orders and three years later became dean of Westbury College. He also gave much of his enormous fortune to the church: too much, in the opinion of the Somerset esquire Thomas Middleton, the father of Canynges's daughter-in-law, Elizabeth. According to Middleton's petition to the royal court of Chancery at Westminster, before the marriage of Elizabeth and John Canynges William had promised his son an inheritance that would make him the richest man in Bristol, but now he was giving away so much of his property that this promise could not be honoured.

Daily [William Canynges] intends to give away more of his livelihood from his son and his heirs and ... not to leave to his said son the tenth part of the goods that he promised to

The first page of an inventory of the contents of St John's church drawn up in 1469. Nearly 350 items are listed, including religious artefacts, service books and vestments. (© DB)

leave him ... as it is plainly noised in the town of Bristol

(Thomas Middleton's Chancery petition, 1467–72)

In addition to its fraternities, chapels, and parish churches, Bristol was ringed about with religious houses: an abbey, and several priories, friaries, and hospitals. Hospitals were run by religious orders and

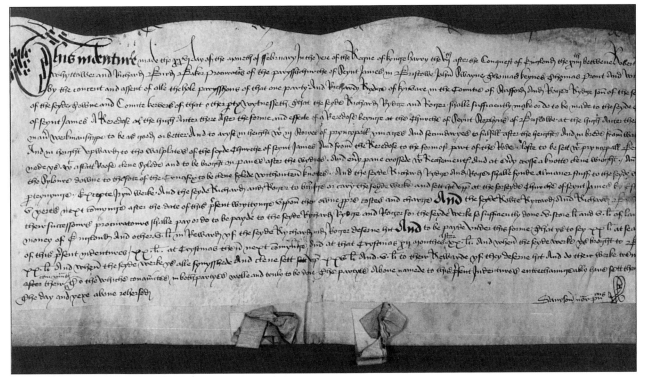

Contract for making a reredos in St James's church dated 1499. (© DB)

had more the character of modern hospices: little could be done for the inmates' physical condition, but at least as important was their spiritual health as they faced the prospect of death. The monks and nuns in abbeys and priories were supposed to remain within their cloisters and spend their time in prayer and meditation. The monasteries and nunneries had been founded by noble families long before the start of our period and were the products of a fashion which had now passed. The townspeople of Cabot's Bristol wanted a form of religion that was more individualistic, closer to their own

lives and more responsive to their needs. The friars provided exactly that. They were not shut up in cloisters but lived and preached among the laity. They were very popular among the Bristol burgesses, who gave generous support to the town's four friaries, one for each order of friars. In their distinctive habits (white for the Carmelites, black for Dominicans, grey for Franciscans and brown for Augustinians) friars would have been a common sight in and around town.

A religious house was not always an oasis of calm. In the early fifteenth century the hospital of St John

Berkeley Chantry Chapel and candelabrum, Bristol Cathedral. The candelabrum is one of the few surviving religious artefacts from pre-Reformation Bristol. (© DB)

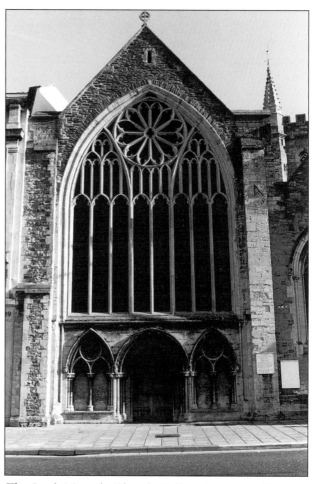

The Lord Mayor's Chapel, College Green, is the only survival of the Hospital of St Mark, or 'The Gaunts', founded in the thirteenth century. It has a splendid medieval interior. (© CM)

the Baptist in Redcliffe was particularly troubled. The ecclesiastical authorities suspected that the hospital was a centre of heresy, and the prior, John St Paul, was found to have allowed the buildings to become dilapidated and to have run up sizeable debts. The problem was so serious that the hospital was taken into crown hands and its management given over to the archbishop of Canterbury and the bishop of Lincoln. Prior St Paul was ordered to relinquish his office. He refused to go, and it took nine years of official pressure – which included cutting off all supplies to the hospital – before he finally submitted in 1413.

Another hospital, St Mark's (the present-day Lord Mayor's Chapel on College Green) did not enjoy good relations with the parish church of St Augustine-the-Less on the other side of the Green. St Mark's had the rights of burial and 'churching' (the

Limoges candlesticks, c. 1230, from the church of St Thomas. These fine examples of the enamelled ware for which Limoges was famous provide further evidence of medieval Bristol's trading links with continental Europe. (© StThom, DB)

Fine alabaster sculptures produced in Nottingham were found in many Bristol churches and homes before the Reformation. This piece depicts St Erasmus being martyred by having his entrails pulled out with a windlass. Behind him, sword in hand, stands the Roman emperor Diocletian, who was responsible for a spate of Christian martyrdoms in the early fourth century. (© CM)

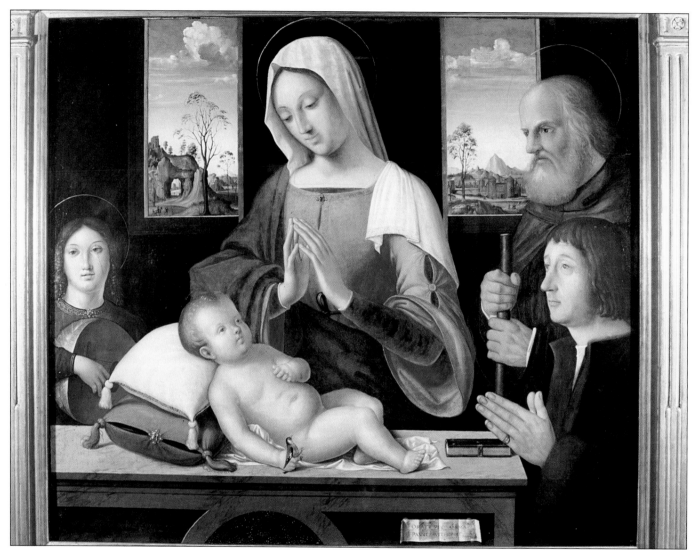

Centre panel of the Withypool Triptych by Antonio Solario, 1514, in the City of Bristol Museum. The triptych was commissioned by Sir Paul Withypool (shown praying), a London merchant with Bristol connections. The side panels (not illustrated) are of St Ursula and St Catherine. (© CM)

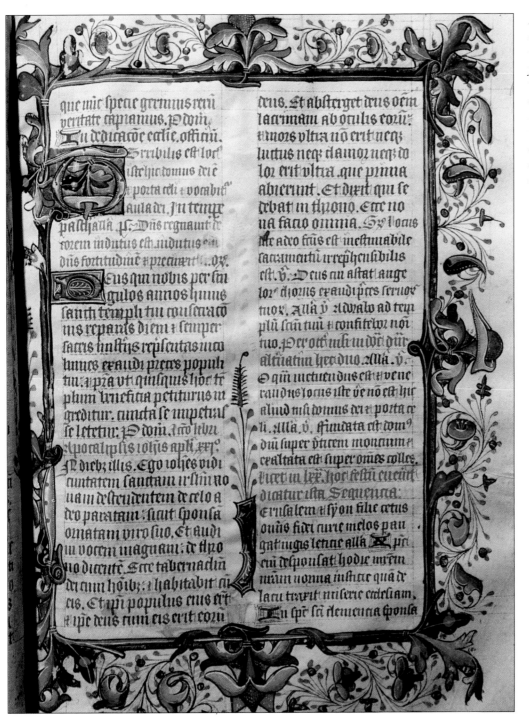

A page of the Sarum missal, c. 1450. Pre-Reformation ritual demanded different texts for certain parts of the service, depending on the time of year when the mass was being celebrated. Developed in Salisbury, the Sarum form of service was the one most commonly used in the south of England. (© CRL)

Two paintings from the Sarum missal. The illustration of the Crucifixion is a fine example of fifteenth-century religious art. St Christopher, a popular saint among medieval travellers, is shown carrying the infant Christ to safety. (© CRL)

ritual purification of mothers after childbirth) of its tenants, despite their being within the parish of St Augustine-the-Less. These rights were important because they brought with them an income from offerings and fees. In 1420 William Chew, vicar of St Augustine-the-Less, enticed a St Mark's tenant who had recently given birth away to St Augustine-the-Less for her churching, thereby receiving candles and the special purification garment that her family were bound to provide to the church in which the ceremony took place. He also removed the bodies of three tenants of St Mark's from the hospital's cemetery and buried them in his own churchyard; by this action he received 100s. paid by their relatives for prayers for their souls. The master of St Mark's took Chew to the bishop's court, which found against him and ordered that the bodies be returned, together with the money, candles and purification garment. Chew refused, and it was only after he had been excommunicated that he finally submitted: the bodies were exhumed and carried to the door of St Mark's with appropriate ceremony, and the money, candles and garment returned.

The greatest Bristol religious community was the Abbey of St Augustine (whose church now forms part of the Cathedral). In common with other great monasteries, the Abbey claimed certain privileges. The most important of these concerned its Liberty, that is the Abbey precinct and its surroundings (roughly, the area now covered by the Cathedral precinct and College Green). The Abbey claimed that the Liberty did not fall within the jurisdiction of Bristol Corporation, but the Corporation maintained that it did. The Abbey also claimed that it could offer sanctuary to criminals. Law-abiding townsfolk were becoming increasingly annoyed at the abuse of sanctuary by criminals who enjoyed its protection

Gateway of St Bartholemew's Hospital, which was founded in the thirteenth century and later became the first home of Bristol Grammar School. (© NHS)

while continuing to perpetrate crimes outside. These two related issues lay at the heart of a series of squabbles between the Abbey and the Corporation that ran through the 1490s, and led to a full-scale riot on College Green (or Abbey Green as it was then known).

We know a great deal about these disputes because the Corporation collected many of the relevant legal documents together in a volume called *The Great White Book*. The account begins with a series of complaints to Henry VII from the Abbot: the mayor had been trying to make the tenants of the Liberty contribute towards taxes levied on the Town and

49

County of Bristol, which, according to the Abbot, did not include the Liberty; the mayor had been holding his own court sessions on the Liberty, which was exempt from his jurisdiction; and he had sent his officers to abduct men from the Abbey's sanctuary and to shut up the shops of those traders in the Liberty who were not Bristol burgesses and who had not paid their tolls as 'strangers', which action the Abbot claimed was illegal because the Liberty was not subject to the restrictions on trade enforced within Bristol proper.

Matters came to a head in 1496. In the early afternoon of Friday 10 June the mayor, William Regent, set off with his officials towards Abbey Green; accompanying him were the wardens of the Bakers' Guild, and in his hands he carried a pair of scales, for the purpose of this expedition was to hold an assize of bread on the Green. This means that the mayor intended to weigh the bread sold by the Abbey tenants, and any baker found selling short measure would be punished by having his bread confiscated and given to the poor. Such an assize was held twice a year within the town walls, and the mayor was determined to demonstrate that the Liberty was subject to exactly the same jurisdiction.

A little earlier, two of the mayor's officers, Henshaw and Brewer, had attempted to make an arrest. Their quarry was Dominick Arthur, a 26-year-old pouchmaker, originally from Limerick. His arrest had been ordered two days earlier following a plea brought against him in the mayor's court, and Arthur had taken sanctuary within the Abbey. Perhaps taking the air on this summer afternoon, he strayed as far as the entrance to the Green by St Augustine-the-Less. This was where Henshaw and Brewer caught him, but Arthur slipped out of his gown and ran off, leaving the mayor's men grasping his empty garment. Brewer threw off his own gown and chased after him, but Arthur reached the Abbey precinct first and shut the gate behind him. A scuffle broke out by the gate, and Brewer was captured and taken to the Abbey Hall. According to Brewer, he was held captive for an hour and threatened with knives and daggers; the Abbot's men, on the other hand, claimed that having accepted their invitation to join them in the Abbey for wine and beer he was asked to put a good word in with the mayor on their behalf and then left on amicable terms.

After his release Brewer ran to meet the mayor's party coming up from the Quay. They made an imposing display: walking before the main party were the town sergeants, then came the mayor, his swordbearer, the sheriff, recorder, town clerk, the wardens of the Bakers' Guild and others, to the number of 25 to 30 men, all in their ceremonial robes. Once they had heard Brewer's story they determined not only to weigh bread, but also to avenge the humiliation of the mayor's officers.

The Abbot's men turned out to meet them. These included servants and workmen employed on the maintenance and rebuilding of the Abbey church, and also some of the monks. One of the monks, it was alleged by the mayor's party, carried a pole axe. The two sides fell to blows. According to witnesses later produced by the Abbot's party, the mayor's men ran amok on the Green: they arrested the cook of the master of St Mark's as he stood in his own doorway with a child in his arms; they pulled down shop fronts and signs; they broke into houses to arrest the occupants, and they attacked innocent bystanders at random. The other side claimed that the Abbot's men lay in wait for them and launched an unprovoked attack with spears, pole axes, stones and staves.

Townspeople gathered on the Quay to watch the mayor's procession now surged up the hill to protect the mayor. Witnesses for the mayor claimed that the mayor had tried to turn back this mob. He seized his ceremonial sword from his swordbearer and brandished it above his head: his supporters later asserted that as he did this he cried 'Keep the peace!' until he was hoarse; his opponents alleged his cry to have been 'Now play we the men!'

Eventually the abbot himself appeared (although according to some accounts only after the mayor's men threatened to burn down the Abbey if Arthur was not given up from sanctuary). He and the mayor met outside St Mark's while the two sides faced each other in uneasy truce. The abbot agreed to surrender his sanctuary man, and delivered him to the mayor, saying, 'Now master mayor here is the man, take him to you and do to him what of right he ought to have'. The mayor thanked the abbot, and in a public display of reconciliation – or possibly surrender on the abbot's part – the two went together to weigh bread on the Green.

This was not the last of the squabbles between the Corporation and the Abbey. In the early sixteenth century, members of the Abbey choir school refused to contribute towards Bristol taxes; as a result, the mayor imprisoned some of the Abbey servants. Then the abbot tried without success to rescue his servants by storming the prison with a 'riotous company' of servants and tenants!

Clearly, relations between the church and the laity were not always harmonious. In addition to tensions between the Corporation and religious communities there were frequent disputes between parishioners and their parish churches over such matters as the nonpayment of tithes, rents owed for church property, or gifts to the church promised but not deliv-

ered, and these might well have led to varying degrees of lay hostility towards the clergy. The church also exercised a degree of control over the private lives of individuals that might today seem intrusive. The church did this through its own system of law and courts which dealt with such matters as marriage, sexual behaviour, and the administration of wills. Offenders were often punished through a combination of penance and public humiliation. Penance could involve fasting, doing good works or repeating certain prayers. Parishioners attending St Mary Redcliffe on 29 May 1519 witnessed an example of punishment by humiliation. Standing before them in the middle of the church was John Mone, a Somerset man who had been convicted of bigamy in the church court: he was dressed only in his undershirt; on his shoulder he bore a bundle of faggots, and he carried a sign which read 'I have deluded the Holy Sacrament of matrimony'. The faggots – or tinder wood – were a none too subtle reminder of the ultimate sanction: the awful punishment of burning alive at the stake. Such drastic measures were re-served for what were considered to be the most heinous crimes: the murder of a husband by his wife or servants; homosexuality; and persistent heresy.

The last of these was a real problem for the authorities. Later medieval England had its own particular brand of heresy, which was called Lollardy. The Lollards took their inspiration from the ideas of a fourteenth-century Oxford theologian called William Wycliffe. They had two central beliefs: that God had already decided which souls would go to Hell and which to Heaven, and so there was no such thing as Purgatory, and no need for good works and prayers for the dead; and that the mass was merely a symbolic gesture, and did not involve the turning of the bread and wine into the body and blood of Christ. Since priests claimed special powers on the basis that only they could officiate at this miracle – or transubstantiation as it is known – the Lollards also held that priests were not a separate caste, and that anyone could officiate at religious ceremonies. This in turn lead some Lollards to translate the Bible from Latin into English in order to break the monopoly that the priests had over its interpretation. They also held that not only lay men, but also women, could preach.

Bristol was notorious as a centre of Lollardy. There were good reasons for this. The national organisation of the church was split into diocese, each under a bishop. Diocesan authority in Bristol was split between the bishop of Bath and Wells and the bishop of Worcester: the dividing line between the two diocese ran along the Avon, so that Redcliffe and Temple was in Bath and Wells diocese, while the rest of the town was in Worcester. It was difficult for either bishop to maintain order, given that it was easy for an offender to slip across the river into the other jurisdiction. Administration north of the river was particularly difficult, owing to the great distance between Bristol and Worcester.

Bristol's success as a commercial and industrial centre, and its good communications, made it fertile ground for Lollardy. In the eyes of the church, just as traders and other travellers had spread the Black Death, a deadly infection of the body, so now they were spreading a plague that infected souls. Lollardy was particularly strong within cloth-making areas, and Bristol's textile industry in Redcliffe and Temple provided it with a ready home. Bristol was associated with Lollardy almost from the very beginning: Wycliffe's disciple John Purvey settled there around the time of his master's death in 1384 and began

recruiting followers from among the town's cloth workers. In 1414 a Lollard knight, Sir John Oldcastle, led a disastrously unsuccessful uprising in London. Bristol provided forty of the rebels, and this was the

The original Temple Church, built by the Knights Templar in the twelfth century, was rebuilt in the fourteenth and fifteenth centuries as a parish church. (© CM)

Interior of the Weavers' Chapel, Temple Church, before the church was gutted in the 1940 Blitz. (© BRO)

largest single contingent among the Lollard rising. After Oldcastle's rebellion the full weight of both church and state was brought to bear on Lollardy. In 1417 proceedings were taken against nine Bristol artisans suspected of Lollardy, including one woman, but they managed to clear themselves after their neighbours testified to their good character.

Lollardy was even found among Bristol clergymen. One such was John Yonge, a chaplain of Temple Church. In 1448, the year in which he was arrested on suspicion of heresy, he was old, frail and blind. He admitted that he had held heretical opinions and that he had spread his ideas among many Bristolians. He submitted himself to the bishop of Bath and Wells for punishment. The bishop declared him a heretic and excommunicated him, thereupon Yonge with difficulty prostrated himself on the floor in a ritual gesture of submission and begged for mercy in the name of God. The bishop, considering his frailty and old age, and his sincere repentance, released him from the sentence of excommunication.

> I have communed knowingly with suspect men and women of errors and heresy in privy places and heard their reading and teaching and given credence and faith to their teaching and favoured them and received them into my house, furthermore I have knowingly possessed English books of errors and heresies ... also I have written and had written divers English books of errors and heresies.
> (John Yonge's confession, 1448, *Register of Thomas Bekynton, Bishop of Bath and Wells*)

Yonge repented and escaped burning, but at least one Bristol heretic, William Smith, was willing to suffer this terrible fate for his beliefs, and in 1457 a former resident of St Catherine's Hospital in Temple Fee was tried for declaring that Smith had died a martyr. Most Lollards preferred to renounce their beliefs and submit themselves to lesser punishment. Fairly typical is the case of John Bouwney of Redcliffe. In 1499 he renounced his Lollardy and was sentenced to parade in only his undershirt, carrying a bundle of faggots, in the cathedral and market-place at Wells and in St Mary Redcliffe, where he was to kneel and say the Lord's Prayer and Ave Maria

five times. In addition, he was not to leave Redcliffe and Temple Fee without the bishop's permission. Some others had to name their Lollard associates as part of their penance.

> William Smyth, who was burnt near to the town of Bristol by the authority of Holy Church for his erroneous opinions, died a true Christian man and a martyr before God.
> (Confession of Walter Comber, 1457, *Register of Thomas Bekynton*)

Bristol retained its notoriety into the sixteenth century. Sir Thomas More remarked that Lollard books were so common in the town that they were 'thrown in the street and left at men's doors by night so that where they would not offer their poison to sell they would of their charity poison men for nothing'. Sir Thomas was exaggerating, but there is evidence of a Bristol trade in heretical books.

By the 1530s the home-grown heresy of Lollardy had been supplemented by radical ideas from the Continent. In Germany, Martin Luther had attacked the Pope and the selling of indulgences, and his stand sparked off a wave of radical agitation across Europe. These protesters – they would later be called 'Protestants' – held ideas that were strikingly similar to those of the Lollards, and it is therefore no surprise that Bristol became an early centre of radical, 'Protestant' agitation. In 1533 the town played host to a 'battle of the pulpits'. Bristol Corporation invited a dynamic young priest called Hugh Latimer to give the sermons at the Preaching Cross on Abbey Green at Lent and Easter that year. Latimer went on to become the Protestant bishop of Worcester, and would end his life at the stake in Oxford, burned by the Catholic Mary Tudor for his beliefs. We do not know what the mayor and common councillors of Bristol were expecting, but in his first course of sermons he attacked the fundamentals of popular Catholic religion: pilgrimages, the intercession of the saints, the veneration of religious images, and possibly belief in Purgatory. All this caused uproar among the more conservative Bristolians. In response, conservative preachers mounted their pulpits in support of these traditional religious practices, and called for Latimer's prosecution as a heretic. The most colourful of these conservatives was William Hubberdyne, whose vigorous style of preaching would later prove fatal: one day while giving a sermon he jumped about so much that his pulpit collapsed and he died of his injuries; when accused of negligence the churchwardens replied that 'they had made their pulpit for preaching, not for dancing'!

The debate between religious radicals and conservatives grew so heated that it came to the attention of Henry VIII's chief minister, Thomas Cromwell, who despatched a commission of investigation to Bristol. A few years earlier Latimer would surely have suffered the same fate as the Lollards, but by 1533 Henry had rejected the authority of the pope because he had refused to allow the king's divorce from Catherine of Aragon, and in this year he married her successor, Anne Boleyn. Both Boleyn and Cromwell were sympathetic to radicals like Latimer, and Henry was very much under their influence: to the horror of Bristol's conservatives, it was Hubberdyne who was sent to the Tower.

Latimer left Bristol after this episode, but the flame he had ignited would not die down. Conflict between radicals and conservatives continued in Bristol throughout the 1530s, and support for the new ideas came from some surprising quarters. Both John Hilsey, prior of the Dominican Friary in Broadmead, and his successor, William Oliver, supported the radicals, despite the fact that their agitation would soon lead to the closure – or dissolution – of all religious houses.

Henry VIII and his radical advisors decided to suppress the religious houses for several reasons: they suspected the monks and nuns of still being loyal to the pope; they wanted to take over their huge monastic estates to provide the hard-pressed government with a financial windfall; and the most radical believed that there was no point to their prime function of praying for souls in Purgatory, since there was no such thing as Purgatory. The Dissolution began in 1536. The smaller religious houses went first. In Bristol that meant institutions like the nunnery of St Mary Magdalene and the four friaries. By this time many of these were already in a state of decay: St Mary's only had one elderly nun and a single novice. The greater houses, like St Augustine's Abbey, held out until the end of the decade. The Abbey was wealthy and in reasonably good order at its dissolution: the only breath of scandal concerned one of the monks, who it was later alleged had run a card school in the precinct to supplement his income from gullible local gamblers.

In effect, the property of the religious houses had been nationalised. Soon, however, the Crown needed money for wars in France, and so much of the former monastic property was sold off: the first 'privatisation'. Bristol Corporation took full advantage of this sell-off, and former church property proved very valuable assets.

Meanwhile, Henry VIII took the opportunity, as self-appointed Head of the Church of England, to rationalise the ecclesiastical structure. Out of the massive and unwieldy diocese of Worcester he carved out a new diocese, Gloucester. At first this

The tomb of Bishop Paul Bush (the first bishop of Bristol) in Bristol Cathedral. Dated 1558, it is a curious mixture of medieval and Renaissance styles: on the one hand it presents Bush as a skeletal cadaver (a later-medieval design intended as a reminder of the inevitability of death), but the design of the canopy and supporting columns is classical, reflecting the influence of the Renaissance. (© DB)

was to include Bristol. Then, in 1542, he decided to create the diocese of Bristol. Perhaps it was lobbying from influential Bristolians that changed his mind, or maybe he realised that it would be nonsensical to allow Gloucester to administer its much larger rival. In any case, the decision was made, and the deserted Abbey church was brought back into service as the Cathedral Church of the Holy and Undivided Trinity. The Cathedral brought a new status to Bristol, that of cathedral city. Since 1373 the Town and County, Bristol was now to be known as the City and County. In 1996, after the 22-year intermission of Avon County, the City and County of Bristol reappeared. The change of name alone does not provide a reason for ending our story in 1542. The Dissolution brought about a massive redistribution of wealth in the city, from the church to the Corporation and the laity. The Reformation brought forth a new religious landscape: henceforth Bristol would be a Protestant city. There were new ideas and new opportunities, and new problems. The year 1542 marks as well as any one year could the end of Bristol's Middle Ages, and the beginning of a new story.

WALKING CABOT'S BRISTOL
Walk One
HOLY HOUSES

This walk takes us in a great arc around the north and east of the old town, and focuses on the houses of monks, nuns and friars which lay just outside the town walls. We also trace part of the course of the Frome, and discover a medieval suburb and a castle. The walk can begin with the stunning view from the top of Brandon Hill, or it can start outside the Cathedral on College Green.

1) BRANDON HILL

Brandon Hill can be reached from Berkeley Square, Charlotte Street or Great George Street. The original name was St Brendan's Hill, from the chapel dedicated to that saint which stood on the hill in Cabot's time. A hermit lived in the chapel. He spent his life in solitary contemplation and prayer: no doubt the climb was sufficiently steep to deter anyone who might otherwise have bothered him. A large cross stood approximately where Cabot Tower now stands, and pilgrims who had returned from the Holy Land said that the hill looked very like Calvary, the hill on which Christ was crucified. Brendan was an Irish monk who died in 578. He is supposed to have set off across the Atlantic in a large coracle, and to have discovered an island paradise: how fitting that in 1897 it was decided to choose his hill for the commemoration of a later Atlantic explorer!

2) ST AUGUSTINE'S ABBEY (THE CATHEDRAL)

From Brandon Hill take the path down to Queen's Parade/Brandon Steep, cross the road and car park to College Street and thence to the Cathedral on College Green. To the west of the central tower the church is Victorian; from the central tower eastwards is late medieval, but there are also earlier features. The church only became a cathedral in 1542; before then it served the monks of St Augustine's Abbey. The Abbey was founded in the twelfth century, but this site may have been a centre of Christianity as far back as the conversion of the pagan Saxons over five hundred years earlier. There is a strong tradition that

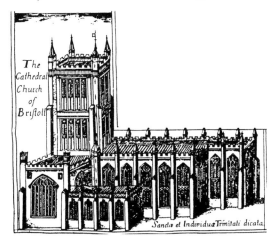

The Cathedral Church of Bristoll

Sancta et Individua Trinitati dicata

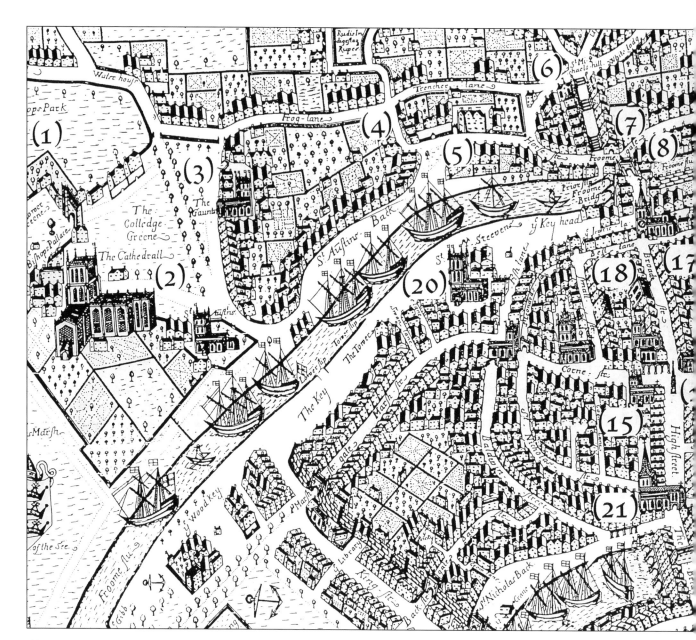

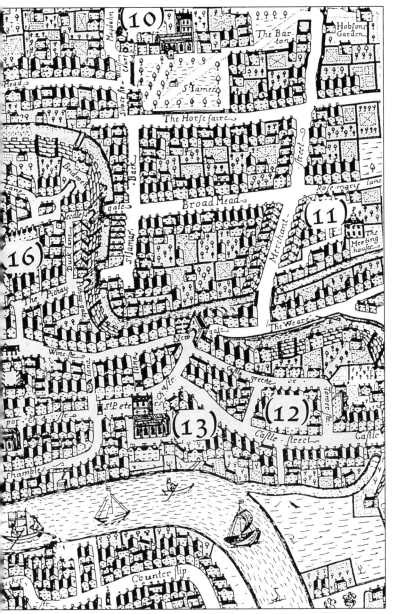

The two plans shown on these and the following pages are taken from Jacobus Millerd's 1673 plan of Bristol. His is the most detailed and accurate depiction of Bristol produced before the eighteenth century. Despite showing Bristol as it was over a century after the end of our period, relatively little had changed in the meantime, and it is still largely the same later medieval and Tudor town. There are only two major differences: the Castle has been replaced by shops and houses, and King Street has been laid out in the reclaimed marshland beyond the town wall. Most of the streets shown on Millerd's plan still exist, so it is still possible to use it as a guide to the walking tour routes around the medieval core of the city.

The numbers in brackets relate to the numbered sections in the walking tours. The first plan relates to Walks One and Two. Walk Three is covered by the second plan.

The illustrations for these walking tours are taken from the pictures of Bristol buildings placed in the margins of Millerd's 1673 plan.

(Plan and line drawings © BRO)

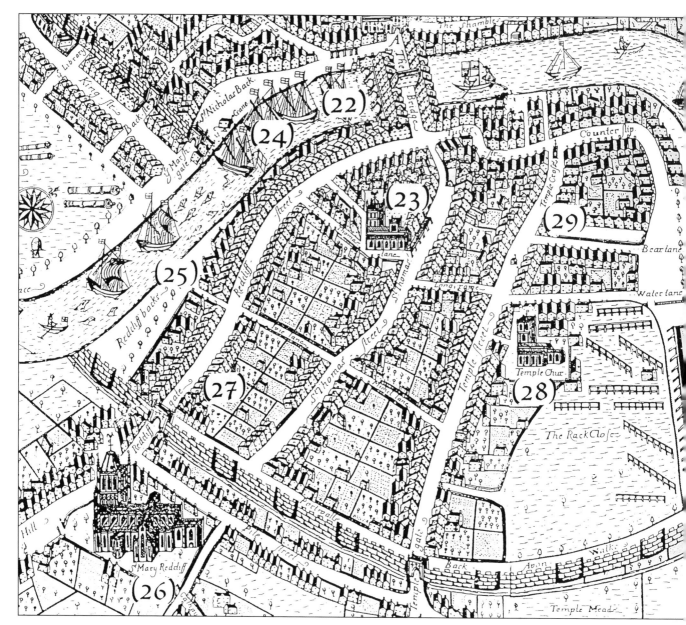

Within the illustration:

(30)

St. Phillips Ch.

Jacobs lane

The Lime kilne

Cold harber

The brick kilne

Kingsmarsh

Avon flu

A prospect of ý great house in Redcliff-str taken from ý Back of Bristoll

Avon flu

61

St Augustine of Canterbury preached here in 603, and that his companion, a monk called Jordan, was buried in what is now College Green, where St Jordan's Chapel stood in Cabot's time. There was very probably a later Saxon church on this site: a stone slab discovered beneath the floor of the Cathedral Chapter House in 1830 and on display inside the Cathedral depicts Christ's 'harrowing of Hell' (saving souls from Hell after the Crucifixion), and was made in about 1050, a few years before the Norman Conquest.

The Abbey of St Augustine (the order of monks took their name from St Augustine of Hippo in North Africa, not St Augustine of Canterbury) was founded in 1140 by Robert Fitzharding, a wealthy and well-connected royal official, who was later created Lord Berkeley. The Berkeleys gave large estates in the surrounding countryside to support the Abbey. Fitzharding's partner in this venture was the future King Henry II, and the fifteenth-century upper storey of the gatehouse has statues of both men and an inscription in their honour. The site was part of Fitzharding's manor of Billeswick (which in Old English means Bill's dairy farm!), and was then open countryside a few minutes' walk from the walled town across the river Frome.

The original church seems to have been built where the Swallow Hotel extension now stands, but this site proved unsuitable (perhaps it was too damp, since it was so close to the undrained marshland where Canon's Marsh is now), and eight years later building began on a new church on the Cathedral site. Impressive remains of this second church can still be seen: the gatehouse arch and Chapter House are superb examples of Norman architecture.

The Abbey continued to enjoy the patronage of the lords of Berkeley Castle, and during the early four-

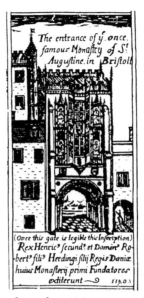

teenth century the eastern end of the church was largely rebuilt. Ambitious building plans were brought to a sudden end by the Black Death of 1348, and about a century was to elapse before large-scale work was resumed, and the central tower was replaced. In Cabot's day a new western end (the nave) was being constructed around the outside of the Norman nave, but the walls had yet to reach as far as the Norman window sills. This work was still unfinished when the Abbey was closed down in 1539. By the time the church reopened in 1542 as the new Cathedral, everything west of the central tower, both the Norman nave and the incomplete curtain of new walls surrounding it, had been demolished. The new Diocese of Bristol was small and very poor, and for many years there was little enthusiasm for church building, so the Cathedral had to wait until the Victorian resurgence of interest in medieval architecture before it could finally be completed.

The church stood at the centre of a whole complex of Abbey buildings, including a dormitory, refectory and hospital for the monks, a granary, bakery, brewery, and stables. The abbot lived in some comfort in his own house, as did his assistant, the prior. During Cabot's stay in Bristol a new priory was built, and the evidence of a recent archaeological excavation has shown just how comfortably the prior lived. The priory had a good system of drains, with inside toilets (or garderobes), decorated floor tiles and expensive ceramic roofing tiles. The Abbey was supplied with fresh water piped from Jacob's Well, and there were flower and herb gardens and a dovecote (for pigeon pie) in the precinct. The bells for the new central tower appear to have been cast on site, since a bell-shaped foundry pit has been unearthed. Archaeologists also found some pieces of fourteenth-century slate which had been inscribed with a sharp pointed tool called a stylus. Some of these were probably used to record the food and drink shipped to the Abbey from its estates: there is even a sketch of a man with a stylus in his hand – presumably stock-taking in the Abbey warehouse – and another which may show one of the flat-bottomed barges, or trows, which were used on the Avon and Severn. There were 28 monks in 1498, and in addition to performing the daily round of prayers they also ran a grammar school and choir school.

In Cabot's time a second church stood close by, on the spot where the first abbey church had stood (the present Swallow Hotel site): the parish church of St Augustine-the-Less. The first church had been built in the 1230s to serve the growing suburb north of the Frome. A substantially new church on this site was finished in the 1480s. In the 1490s the vicar of St Augustine-the-Less taught in the Abbey schools.

3) ST MARK'S HOSPITAL (LORD MAYOR'S CHAPEL)

Cross the Green towards Park Street. In Cabot's day we would pass St Jordan's Chapel and the Preaching Cross, where public sermons were given at Easter and Lent. The Green was used by the Abbey as its cemetery, so the skeletons of numerous monks and their servants must lie beneath our feet. On the other side, the Lord Mayor's Chapel is all that remains of St Mark's Hospital. The Hospital was founded in the thirteenth century by Maurice de Gaunt, great-grandson of Robert Fitzharding, the founder of St Augustine's, and Maurice's nephew, Robert de Gourney (their tombs can be seen inside the south aisle chapel). Maurice's younger brother Henry was its first master. The Hospital was set up to feed 100 poor every day, but by the early fifteenth century this was no longer the practice. Instead, twenty-seven poor men lived within the Hospital. This was far less of a burden to the house, which had declined since the Black Death of 1348, but the Hospital's charter of foundation clearly required the brethren to feed 100 poor, so the document was altered to make it appear that the new practice had been the original purpose of the founders. By Cabot's day even this limited commitment to poor relief seems to have been abandoned. While the Hospital may have been but a shadow of its former self, there was still money to build new houses on the Green in the 1470s (perhaps as an investment), to rebuild the eastern end of the chapel, to replace the great window facing the street, and in 1487 to build the present tower.

Despite its problems, St Mark's continued to be patronised by the Berkeleys – the fine fifteenth-century tomb of Sir Maurice and Lady Berkeley of Stoke Gifford stands in the chancel – and Miles Salley, bishop of Llandaff (who claimed kinship with the Berkeleys) paid for some of the rebuilding and was buried in 1516 under another fine tomb near the Berkeleys. In addition, Sir Robert Poyntz of Iron Acton (died 1520) had an impressive chantry chapel built here, with Spanish floor tiles added by his son Sir Francis and the arms of Henry VIII and Catherine of Aragon on the ceiling. Also worth looking out for is a fragment of late-medieval wall painting, and the tomb of a mid-fourteenth-century merchant, with an inscription which incorrectly claims it to be of Henry de Gaunt. By the 1530s it seems that the Hospital's only guests were retired gentlefolk. When it was closed down in 1539 the community was made up of only the master and four brothers, together with sixteen servants and choristers. The Corporation bought the site in 1541, and in 1721 it became the official place of worship of the mayor and Corporation. Much of the stained glass was bought by the Corporation in the nineteenth century, and so while some of it is contemporary with Cabot, it would not have been here in his day.

Walking up Park Street and turning right down Unity Street/Orchard Street brings us into what was the hospital precinct. This stretched down to St Augustine's Back and Frogmore Street (the latter means frog pool and with nearby Frog Lane suggests that this was a marshy area with lots of pond life!). Orchard Street and Culver Street (from an old word for dovecote or pigeon-house) remind us that this eighteenth-century development was built over the hospital gardens. Piped water was supplied from springs on Brandon Hill. Until the middle of the twentieth century a winged lion (the symbol of St Mark) stood on the corner of Frogmore Street and Pipe Lane, and this may once have been a boundary marker for the hospital precinct.

4) THE KEY (QUAY)

Walk up Orchard Avenue, turn right into Frogmore Street and then right again into Pipe Lane. Pipe Lane takes its name from a water conduit that still runs under present-day Park Street. Standing at the junction of Pipe Lane and Colston Street and looking down towards St Augustine's Parade, we would have seen, in Cabot's day, a busy dockside.

Underneath the roads and gardens of the Centre the Frome still runs. The river was covered over as far as Narrow Quay to accommodate the pre-war tram centre. Cabot would have known this as the Key, that part of the town docks from which the big sea-going vessels sailed, and his own *Matthew* probably sailed from here in 1497. The course of the Frome here is in fact man-made; originally, the river curved south-eastwards, roughly parallel to St Stephen's Street and Baldwin Street, and joined the Avon on Welsh Back. The present channel was dug in the 1240s: a remarkable feat of medieval engineering. This provided a wide deep-water dock, and allowed the town to expand southwards. At the same time the marshes of Lewin's Mead were drained, allowing northward expansion, and new town walls built.

Facing us on the other side of the dock in Cabot's day would have been the elegant stone customs house, where the two royal customs officials worked to ensure that the various tolls on merchandise shipped through Bristol were paid to the king. Nearby was an equally impressive stone conduit house, which supplied spring water piped from Boiling Well in Ashley Vale to both houses and ships. The thirteenth-century town walls extended as far as King Street (a tower can still be seen inside St Nicholas's Almshouse) and ran along the quayside. The wall towers were being converted into

fashionable town houses, like the great Viell's Tower that stood at the beginning of Clare Street. The houses along this street had overhanging arcades, like the Rows in Chester, so that one could walk from the Key to St Leonard's Gate without getting wet in bad weather. To our right, by Broad Quay, the wall was pierced by a double watergate: two tunnels ran through the eight-foot (2.4-m) thick wall and sloped down to the river. They may have led to a dry dock, or to slipways where vessels could be unloaded at low tide (the waterways of the Severn Estuary have an enormous tidal reach (the difference between high and low tide) and until the docks were 'floated' or regulated by locks in the early nineteenth century the tidal reach here was 10 metres).

Turning left into Colston Street brings us to the site of the Carmelite Friary.

5) THE CARMELITE FRIARY

In Cabot's time there was a large Carmelite Friary where Colston Hall now stands. The Friary was founded by the future Edward I in 1267. This house of the White Friars was the most impressive of the four Bristol friaries: the church was 180 feet long, and its tower and spire was 200 feet high (about the same height as St Mary Redcliffe's spire); the cloister, where the friars walked in bad weather, was about 80 feet square. Behind the house was a huge garden that stretched up the side of the hill to where the Red Lodge now stands, and a large cistern collected water from the 'Park Street' conduit and from there it was piped into the centre of Bristol. However, by the time of the Dissolution the Friary was in a sorry state: the prior and sexton had fled before the royal commissioners reached the house, having stolen and sold off much of its wealth. Only four poor friars

were left when it was suppressed in 1538. On this site in the 1570s Sir John Young built a town mansion so big that it was known simply as 'The Great House': Red Lodge was one of two lesser houses built in its back garden. Queen Elizabeth I stayed here on her famous visit in 1574. In 1867 the Great House was replaced by the Colston Hall. Look up the hill slightly towards Host Street. This is a corruption of 'Horse Street', so called because this was the gentler way down to the river Frome, and so was used by horses. To see how intrepid or foolhardy pedestrians got down to the river, we shall carry on up the hill until we reach the junction with Lower Park Row.

6) STEEP ST (CHRISTMAS STEPS)

The steps leading off from the street were built in the seventeenth century: the plaque in the wall tells their story. Before then, this was known as Steep Street, for obvious reasons. In wet or icy weather this would have been particularly dangerous. The impressive building next to us is Foster's Almshouse. The existing almshouse is Victorian, but the chapel is original, and dates to around 1504. The almshouse was founded by John Foster, a wealthy Bristol merchant. The chapel is dedicated to the Three Kings of Cologne (their (modern) statues can be seen in niches on the front of the chapel). The dedication was doubtless inspired by Cologne Cathedral, which is also dedicated to the Three Kings who brought gifts to the infant Christ, but there is no record of Foster having travelled to Germany. Steep Street used to continue right up to the top of St Michael's Hill. St Michael's Church, whose tower is just visible if we look up towards the hill, is eighteenth century, but this replaces a medieval church on the same spot. Opposite the church, where the King David Hotel now stands, was the priory of St Mary Magdalene, a nunnery founded by Eva, the widow of Robert Fitzharding in about 1173. By the time of its dissolution in 1536 it had only two nuns, an elderly nun and a young novice, and two servants. The priory has gone, but it has given its name to Maudlin Street that runs past it.

At the top of St Michael's Hill, near where Cotham Parish Church now stands, was a public well with a stone enclosure. Near that was a gibbet where criminals were put to death, and a plaque in the wall of the church commemorates the burning here of Protestant martyrs under Mary Tudor. The condemned's last sight was intended to be a large stone cross, set next to the gallows: the base has been incorporated into the churchyard wall, and is marked by another plaque.

7) ST BARTHOLOMEW'S HOSPITAL

Walk down Christmas Steps (look out for the two old statues high on the wall to our right as we do so) and turn left at the bottom. A medieval-looking arch forms the entrance to the NHS offices. This was once St Bartholomew's Hospital. This is not a public right of way, but it is usually possible to enter the courtyard during office hours: please ask permission first. The hospital was founded by Sir John de la Warre of Brislington, probably soon after the new Frome channel was cut in the 1240s, when this area was drained and reclaimed. The religious community established here to look after the old, poor and sick had an eventful history. In 1285 the master was murdered by two chaplains from St James's Priory. There was further trouble in the next century. Both men and women made up the religious community, and in the 1330s the sisters expelled the brethren and

the master and elected a prioress; the bishop of Worcester forced the women to allow back their male colleagues in 1386, but the women tried to rid themselves of the brethren again, unsuccessfully, in 1412. Perhaps in part to put a stop to this conflict, in 1445 the Corporation and the de la Warres refounded the hospital as the Fraternity of St Clement, charged with looking after twelve poor sailors. By this time the buildings were gravely dilapidated.

In 1531 Lord de la Warre, the original founder's descendant, gave the site to the Bristol merchant Robert Thorne, and with his brother Nicholas he founded the Bristol Grammar School here (although the school may originally have been housed in a tower on Frome Gate). The site was excavated in the 1970s. The excavation revealed evidence of weaving being practised on this site. A number of skeletons were found of old men and women suffering from osteoporosis, leg ulcers, bed sores and anaemia, much as one would expect among the inmates of a medieval hospital. An information panel in the first courtyard gives an indication of the likely internal layout (a second panel in the far courtyard gives information on the reclamation of this area in the 1240s): as well as the chapel, evidence for a hall and kitchen has been found. The medieval stonework of the entrance passage presents problems. The inner arcade of round Norman arches predates the founding of the Hospital itself; if this was built on reclaimed land the stonework would have to have been brought here from elsewhere. Similarly, the thirteenth-century stonework of the outer entrance is not in its original position, since the medieval floor level was much lower than the present level of this entrance way. It has been suggested that this later stonework, together with the mutilated statue of the Virgin Mary and infant Christ, was brought here from the Carmelite Friary after its dissolution: it is of roughly the right date, and a statue of the Virgin and Child in the Carmelites' garden wall was a well-known landmark in Cabot's day.

Turn left out of St Bartholomew's and continue until St John's Church and Gate appears across the road to our right.

8) FROME BRIDGE

At this spot Cabot would have seen the twin towers and gate of the northern end of Frome Bridge. This was a stone, two-arched structure with a gateway at each end protected by twin towers. The distance between the two gates was about forty feet. Houses and a school were built into these towers. A conduit carried fresh water from Kingsdown across the bridge and into the town centre. The gatehouse at the southern end of the bridge was part of the new town wall built after the reclamations of the 1240s. Next to the bridge the wall was pierced by a tunnel leading to a watergate with a stone cross above it (perhaps like that on Broad Quay). On the south bank was an almshouse founded by the merchants William Spencer and William Canynges. On the north bank was a wooden jetty where boats coming downriver could unload supplies for the inhabitants of Lewin's Mead.

9) THE GREYFRIARS

The large office block ahead of us on Lewin's Mead, called 'Greyfriars', is built on the site of the Franciscan Friary, founded about the same time as St Bartholomew's in the 1240s. The land may have been given by St James's Priory. The Friary was rebuilt in the 1380s. In Cabot's time it consisted of a church, over 160 feet long with two aisles and a bell tower, a

cloister, a hall, kitchen and other domestic rooms, some of which were supplied with garderobes (lavatories), together with dovecotes, gardens, orchards, fishponds, a cemetery and limekilns. The buildings were of high quality: excavations in the 1970s found the remains of stained glass, pennant stone roof tiles, and ceramic floor tiles and roof-ridge crests. What may have been the kitchen and refectory block stood until the nineteenth century: it was a well-built stone building of two floors with a wooden half-round or 'wagon' roof.

Part of the stone wall supporting the river cliff behind the site is medieval, and a storage 'cupboard' has been found carved into the stonework. On top of the cliff was another stone building, perhaps used as a guesthouse. The Friary's water supply came from a lead conduit which ran down the cliff face from Kingsdown. There was a water pump in the middle of the cloister garden. The water-logged site preserved a wealth of organic material: archaeologists found wooden bowls, platters and spatulas, as well as fashionable pointed-toed leather shoes. A clay watering-pot, with holes in its bottom, was also found, together with slates which were probably used in the Friary school: 'BRISTOLL' was inscribed on one, 'FR HENRIC(I)U(S)' ('Brother Henry') on another. Schools were often attached to friaries, and teaching was sometimes at an advanced level. The graves of forty people of both sexes have also been found, including a family vault suggesting that in common with many other friaries Greyfriars was a popular resting place for the laity. By its dissolution in 1538 Greyfriars was in debt and had only six friars.

10) ST JAMES'S PRIORY

Either cross the road and go along Christmas Street,

through St John's Gate and up Broad Street to end the tour here, or continue along Lewin's Mead until you reach the junction with Lower Maudlin Street. Stop here and turn right, looking back across Rupert Street towards Bridewell Street. Here Cabot would have seen a large square tower and Monk's Bridge, so called because it allowed visitors to St James's Priory to cross the Frome. The tower used to house the town prison, but in 1449–50 this was moved to Newgate, at the east end of town, and by Cabot's time the tower had been converted into fashionable town houses.

Turn around and go up Lower Maudlin Street. On Whitson Street we come to the gate of St James's Priory. In Cabot's time the precinct boundary walls of Greyfriars and St James's Priory faced each other across Lower Maudlin Street. A pre-Conquest church may have existed on this site, but the Benedictine Priory was founded between 1129 and 1137 by Robert Fitzroy, earl of Gloucester, the illegitimate son of Henry I. Before the main body of the church was completed, Robert built a chapel here using stone left over from his rebuilding of Bristol Castle. The Priory was a cell (that is, a subsidiary branch) of Robert's greater foundation of Tewkesbury Abbey. What remains is largely post-medieval, but the west front with its circular window and inside the great round piers or columns of the two arcades separating the nave from the side aisles are original. The cloister was built where the bus station now stands, and recent excavations have revealed a large cemetery to the east of the church. In Cabot's time the nave was used by the local people as their parish church. In 1374 the parishioners paid for a new bell tower. Three chantry chapels were established here, including one, for William Pownam, founded as late as 1545, less than three years before all chantries were

abolished! At the Dissolution the Priory church's dual status as parish church saved it from destruction. No more than four monks remained in 1539, and the domestic buildings were sold off to a wealthy London tailor, who built himself a mansion on the site. The church is now occupied by the Little Brothers of Nazareth. It is open to the public, but as a place of worship: please respect this.

11) THE DOMINICAN FRIARY

Return to Lewin's Mead, cross the road (carefully!) to The Horsefair, and continue as far as Merchant Street. We are in Broadmead, a typical post-war shopping precinct. However, this began life as a medieval suburb, laid out by the earls of Gloucester in the twelfth century. The main grid pattern of streets is largely intact. Just beyond the junction of Horsefair and Merchant Street (the latter street name dates back to Cabot's time) is Barr's Court. In the fifteenth century this is where a bar, or barrier, blocked this main route into town. This was used to keep undesirables out of town: Corporation ordinances decreed that no prostitutes were allowed beyond the Bar.

Turn right down Merchant Street and then left into Quakers' Friars. The first part of this name commemorates seventeenth and eighteenth-century Quakers, whose meeting-house still stands on this spot, but the second part brings us to the third of the Bristol friaries, that of the Dominican, or Black Friars. The friars' church has completely disappeared, but the building now occupied by the Registry Office once formed three sides of the cloister. The Friary was founded by Maurice de Gaunt (founder of St Mark's) and his kinsman Matthew de Gournay in about 1227–8. Part of the original roof survives, and is the oldest timber roof in Bristol. Like the Greyfriars, the Dominicans ran a school and many Bristol people left instructions to be buried in their cemetery.

12) THE CASTLE

Return to Merchant Street and continue as far as Broad Weir. The weir, or small dam, diverted water from the Frome, which now runs under the Galleries shopping centre, to feed a moat which encircled the east end of Castle Park. In Cabot's day, we would now be looking across this moat to a massive castle. The Normans erected a wooden castle on this site, to block off the only landward approach to Bristol. Then, in the 1120s, Robert earl of Gloucester began building what would become one of the finest stone castles in England, with a massive central tower or keep similar to Rochester Castle keep or the White Tower of the Tower of London. By Cabot's time the

Castle was garrisoned by only a handful of people and its buildings were in disrepair. Most of it was pulled down on the orders of Oliver Cromwell in 1656 and the site was redeveloped for houses and shops. If you want to know more about the Castle, follow the trail around Castle Park and read the information panels: there are still things to see above ground, and you can inspect the foundations of the keep revealed by the 1989 excavation.

Turn right and walk along Broad Weir towards the Galleries. In Cabot's day the Castle Mills straddled the channel that connected the river to the moat. These were two watermills housed in one large building, and were used for grinding corn. The profits of the Castle Mills were used to support St James's Priory. Next, on his left, Cabot would have seen the massive Newgate, a fortified gateway at the town end of the Castle drawbridge that spanned the north-west corner of the moat. There was once a grammar school in the northern wing of Newgate, but Cabot would have known this building as the town prison.

13) ST PETER'S CHURCH

This is the gutted church on our left, a victim of the Blitz which caused massive devastation to this area. The present church is later medieval, but a Saxon church stood on this site, which is close to the first settlement of Bristol. The St Peter's that Cabot knew served a densely settled area between the Castle and the eastern town wall, including several fashionable houses. William Canynges owned fourteen shops here, and in his will of 1474 he left money for the building of a public water fountain on the corner of present-day Dolphin Street and St Peter's Street, on the site of an ancient holy well dedicated to St Edith.

Between the church and the Avon was the magnificent St Peter's Hospital, which was still in use as a workhouse in the nineteenth century. This walk ends here, but if you continue along the road to the Wine Street–Corn Street–Broad Street–High Street junction you will be at the beginning of the second walk.

WALKING CABOT'S BRISTOL
Walk Two
THE TOWN WALLS

This walk takes us in a circuit around most of the original town walls. Along the way we discover the sites of eleven churches, a pillory and a synagogue, and learn something of what lies beneath our feet.

14) CHRIST CHURCH (HOLY TRINITY)

Part of Chriſt Church

The ſouth proſpect of y High Croſs in Briſtoll

We begin at the spot where Bristol's High Cross used to stand, at the junction – or carfax – of the four principal streets of the medieval town centre: High Street, Broad Street, Wine Sreet and Corn Street. This was the pivot around which turned the commercial and political life of Cabot's Bristol. The High Cross was taken to Stourhead (Wilts) in the eighteenth century, but it is remembered in a plaque on the corner of Corn Street and Broad Street, and a replica of the upper part of the cross stands in Berkeley Square. A cross on this site may have been erected to commemorate the granting of county status in 1373, but the earliest part of the present High Cross was probably built in the fifteenth century. Market stalls were set up around the base of the cross, and it was sometimes the scene of public executions.

Four churches stood close to each corner of the carfax. Christ Church was more commonly known as Trinity Church in Cabot's day. What we see now is an eighteenth-century rebuilding: little, if anything, is left of the medieval church. Opposite Christ Church across Broad Street was St Ewen's. This had a great east window facing on to Broad Street, and one aisle was used by the Tailors' Guild as their chapel (St John-on-the-Wall, close to the Tailors' Guild Hall in Tailors' Court, and dedicated to John the Baptist, the tailors' patron saint, was too small to accommodate the guild chapel). Between St Ewens and Corn Street

The ſouth proſpect of the Tolzey of Briſtoll

was the Council House and Tolsey. The Tolsey was an arcade, open to the street on one side, where the mayor held his court: in such a public spot, justice could be seen to be done, in one sense at least, and no doubt exposure to the elements speeded up the process of law! Offices for the legal staff were contained in the Council House behind (the present building, the 'Old' Council House, was built in the 1820s). Near the junction of High Street and Wine Street, and now partially concealed by the Norwich Union building, stands the blitzed shell of St Mary-le-Port. A church stood on this site in Saxon times, but what's left is largely fourteenth and fifteenth century. The 'port' element in the name comes from an old word for a market-place: once, Bristol's main market was held in front of the church door. By Cabot's day the market was no longer held here, but the spot was far from tranquil: close by was Haddon's tannery, which must have produced some pretty noxious odours!

15) ALL SAINTS' CHURCH

This is the fourth of the 'carfax churches'. The western end of the church, facing All Saints' Lane, is Norman (the church was in existence by 1140), but the rest was rebuilt, partly at the expense of the parishioners, from the 1420s to the 1440s. The tower was replaced in the eighteenth century. Running along the Corn Street side of the church was another Tolsey. This was probably used as a commercial exchange rather than as a court of law. The famous 'nails' outside the eighteenth-century Exchange are no earlier than the sixteenth century, but merchants had been doing deals along this side of Corn Street long before this.

At the end of the church by the junction of All Saints' Lane and Corn Street was a water fountain. At this end of the church two houses were erected either side of the west door in the 1430s and '40s. The southern of the two was a house for the parish clergy; the other (rebuilt in the eighteenth century and now a café) housed the Fraternity of Kalends (see p. 43 for an account of this). In All Saints' Lane an almshouse for eight poor women was founded in 1350, and the lane around the back of the church (which is usually open during the day) was where the Cooks' Guild had their shops: this was the place to come for medieval 'fast food' (one speciality was salmon sold by the slice).

Looking back along Corn Street, Cabot would have seen yet another church, that of St Werburgh's, on the corner of Small Street. This was about 60 feet square, with a very handsome bell tower. The church was demolished and rebuilt on Mina Road in 1879 (the present tower is from the medieval church) and gave its name to the district.

16) PITHAY

Walk along Wine Street until we reach Pithay on our left. At this point Cabot would have seen the 'House of Justice and Correction' standing in the middle of the street. This was a squat, stone building with iron bars on the windows and a wooden pillory above. This was where lesser wrongdoers (such as bakers found guilty of selling under-weight bread) were held before being beaten or exposed on the pillory.

Turn into Pithay. At the junction of Pithay and Tower Lane was Aylward's Gate, part of the pre-thirteenth-century town wall; this gate had been partially demolished in Cabot's time, since the old wall had been superseded by the new one running beside the rerouted Frome. One of the old towers had been converted into a house. Walking along Tower Lane, we can see how it still follows the sweep of the old wall. Notice also the parish boundary markers on the wall to our left. Pithay means 'enclosed pit or well', and refers to a well within a stone enclosure, with a tiled roof. This was close to the parish boundary. Wine Street is a corruption of Winch Street, and may have derived its name from the winch used to draw buckets in the well (alternatively, it may refer to the device used to winch offenders up onto the pillory!). Close to the well (perhaps a little too close for modern hygiene requirements) were male and female public lavatories. Off John Street (originally St John Street) the almshouse of Mayor Robert Strange had been newly built when Cabot arrived in Bristol. A little further on, at the end of John Street, was Blind Gate, another entrance in the old wall.

17) TAILORS' COURT

Before reaching John Street, turn left underneath Fitzharding House into Tailors' Court. This is an unusually well-preserved medieval courtyard. Land fronting a main street was expensive, and so plots tended to have narrow frontages with long back-yards: fronting the street would be a shop with living rooms above and a workshop or hall behind; in the yard behind this would be other workshops, stables, kitchens and warehouses.

Immediately to our right as we emerge into the court is the churchyard of St John-on-the-Wall. This land was sold to the church for this purpose by the owner of the adjoining tenement in 1390, against the wishes of St James's Priory (who up until then had enjoyed the burial fees paid by St John's parishioners who used their cemetery) and the Tailors' Guild, whose hall looked onto Tailors' Court (perhaps they had a claim on the land, or did not want a burial ground so close to their hall). The eighteenth-century Tailors' Guildhall is on our right at the far end of the court (notice the shell hood over the door, with its depiction of the head of St John the Baptist (the tailors' patron saint) on a plate, as requested by Salome), and across the Broad Street entrance is a medieval timber-framed house: notice the statues in the lower part of the wall (of St Michael and St George?) and the pointed arched doorway or window.

The Tower Lane end of the court has been excavated. The remains of a fine Norman stone house were found, which may have belonged to Robert Fitzharding, founder of St Augustine's Abbey (hence Fitzharding House); remains of a stable or storehouse, contemporary with Cabot, were also found at this end. Among other finds were fifteenth-century trade tokens from Venice and Germany, tin-glazed bowls from Spain, and a bottle stopper made from a horse's tooth.

18) BROAD STREET

From Tailors' Court we enter Broad Street. Right in front of us is the Victorian Guildhall, built on the site of its medieval predecessor. This was the main meeting place for the Corporation. Next door was the chapel of St George, founded by Richard Spicer (mayor of Bristol in 1371) for the burgesses' use: in effect, the precursor of the Lord Mayor's Chapel. The building at number 43's Georgian façade hides a late-medieval tenement, and other medieval remains lurk behind more modern frontages along this street. Most of Bristol's medieval houses had stone dividing walls to prevent the spread of fire: Bristol never had the equivalent of the Great Fire of London, and has a greater number of medieval domestic buildings surviving. Beneath our feet is a maze of medieval cellars. Large vaulted cellars were built under most of the major town centre streets: there were twenty under both Broad Street and Corn Street, and over thirty under High Street. Many still survive, and a few have been converted into restaurants or bars (the cellars at Harvey's Restaurant and Museum are the most famous). Sleds were preferred over carts for transporting goods in Bristol, perhaps because the

sleds' runners spread the weight more evenly than did wheels, and so were less likely to cause the roadway to collapse into a cellar.

At the northern end of Broad Street is the church of St John the Baptist, or St John-on-the-Wall. Like several other Bristol churches, St John's was built along the length of the town wall and incorporated a gateway; it is now unique in Bristol. The church was rebuilt through the generosity of Mayor Walter Frampton, who died in 1388. Above the gateway are the statues of Brennius and Bellinus, mythical Trojan princes who were supposed to have founded Bristol after the Greeks had taken Troy with their wooden horse; the figures look post-medieval (their niches probably contained images of saints John and Lawrence originally), but the story seems to have been believed in Cabot's day. The two smaller arches either side of the main gateway were made long after Cabot's time, to ease the flow of traffic. Standing under the central arch, we can see the slot for the portcullis, a metal frame which was lowered to seal the gateway, and the blocked original entrance to the church. Where the entrance is now Cabot would have seen a single-storey stone annexe: another conduit house, supplying spring water brought across the Frome Bridge in lead pipes. Tributaries of the main pipes were called feathers, because they were supposed to be the width of a swan feather: one document in the city archives, an agreement to supply water through such a tributary, still has a swan feather attached! The conduit has been moved to the other side of the wall, in Nelson Street, and continued to supply water until very recently. Nelson Street was a dark narrow alley in Cabot's day, and was called Grope Lane, because it was not possible for two people to pass each other without touching! Inside the church we can see the impressive tomb of Walter Frampton and the fifteenth-century brass of Thomas Rowley and his wife. There are also fragments of medieval stained glass in the windows. The Chancel (eastern end) had been added shortly before Cabot's arrival. The lower vault or crypt was practically a separate church, and housed the Fraternity of the Holy Cross, founded in 1465.

19) BELL LANE AND LEONARD LANE

Walking along Bell Lane takes us past the site of a vanished medieval church, St Lawrence's. Like St John's, this was built along the length of the wall, and both churches originally shared the tower over St John's Gate. There may have been a nunnery on this site before St Lawrence's was built. St Lawrence's was deconsecrated and sold off in 1580 and eventually demolished in 1824, but it is remembered in the name of the office block overlooking Bell Lane.

Almost immediately after passing St Lawrence's, Cabot would have found himself at yet another church, St Giles'. Like St John's, this incorporated a gateway, this one giving access to the Key from Small Street. Before 1290, when the Jews were expelled from England, this part of town was the Jewish quarter, and on this site stood a synagogue. After 1290 parts of the synagogue were used as cellars, but Cabot could still have seen remains of the upper levels between St Giles' and St Lawrence's churches (recent excavations have uncovered a Jewish ritual bath, or mikveh, on Jacob's Wells Road). The Assize Courts to our left on Small Street are built on the site of a Norman stone hall, which was converted into separate chambers in the early sixteenth century.

Crossing Small Street, we enter a tunnel, St Leonard's Lane (look out for the old stone face above the entrance as we do so). We are still following the line of the town wall, and some of the timbers above our head may be medieval: there were a number of small alleys like this, with houses built over the top, in the increasingly crowded medieval town centre. The town wall to our right would have been about forty feet high and eight feet thick, with a walkway along the top. Originally, there would have been a ditch on the other side, but much of this was probably filled in by Cabot's day to allow houses to be built against the outside of the wall; indeed, the old inner circuit of walls had probably been demolished in many places, or incorporated into later buildings. Very soon we come to a doorway on our right: going through here, and down the steps, brings us to St Stephen's Street.

20) ST STEPHEN'S CHURCH

This may once have been a cell of Glastonbury Abbey which was converted into a parish church: the abbey had the right of patronage (the appointment of priests) of the church in Cabot's day. The parish and church of St Stephen's was created after the diversion of the Frome in the thirteenth century allowed a new suburb to develop here on reclaimed marshland in the angle between the old and the new town walls. Pile Street, where St Stephen's Street now runs, may have been named after the wooden piles driven into the marsh to provide firm foundations for building, and Cabot's contemporaries could remember the discovery, while digging deep foundations for a house on this street, of articles of clothing and timber, perfectly preserved in the waterlogged soil. This became a prosperous area: Marsh Street, leading from the stile at the edge of St Stephen's churchyard down to Marsh Gate on the new wall (the present-day King Street) was the home of many rich merchants.

Huic Turris pae vix repetitur

The South prospect of S.t Steevens Church in Bristoll

In the 1470s the church was largely rebuilt, at the expense of the wealthy parishioners and Glastonbury Abbey. Mayor John Shipward, whose house was close by, paid for the new tower and east window. In a great storm in 1703 the top of the tower crashed into the body of the church, and the church as we see it today has been restored several times since; however, its last restoration, finished in 1898, left its exterior looking very much as Cabot would have known it. The crown (or pierced stone parapet) at the top of the tower, a West Country speciality, is particularly striking, as is the vaulted porch. Inside, the nave was divided with screens of carved and gilded oak into between five and nine chantry chapels, each with its own altar, and sumptuously appointed with plate and rich vestments. This was a church designed not for preaching, but as a prayer factory for the souls of rich benefactors. The two fourteenth-century tombs may be those of Edmund Blanket and Walter Tyddesley and their wives. The former was a wealthy clothier, but unfortunately it is highly unlikely that he gave his name to the blanket, although he may have taken his name from the type of cloth he dealt in ('blanquette' was a name given to any white cloth). Tyddesley was MP for Bristol in 1385.

21) ST NICHOLAS'S CHURCH

Walking from the junction of St Stephen's Street with Clare Street into Corn Street takes us through what in Cabot's day would have been another church built over a town-wall gate: St Leonard's. This did not enjoy the wealth of benefactions showered on St Stephen's or St John's, but was still a substantial building, nearly sixty feet long and thirty feet wide, with an imposing main gateway and smaller gates over Pile Street and Baldwin Street.

Turning right down St Nicholas Street brings us back on the inside of the original town wall: the block between St Nicholas and St Stephen/Baldwin streets follows the sweep of the old wall. Cabot rented an expensive house on St Nicholas Street, and he and his family no doubt worshipped at St Nicholas's church, on our right at the end of the street. This is the fourth of our gateway churches, with a twenty-foot-wide gatehouse (demolished in the eighteenth century because it obstructed traffic) built into its east end linking High Street with Bristol Bridge. The upper part of the church was rebuilt in the eighteenth century, and the church was gutted during the Blitz, but the lower church, or crypt, is fourteenth century, and the fifteen-foot-thick town wall forms its southern wall. Like the crypt of St John's, this was virtually a separate church, with its own fraternity, of the Holy Cross. A pig market was held near here, perhaps on the site of the eighteenth-century market.

By the church door is a flight of steps. Here was a

door through the town wall and steps down to Baldwin Street. The area within the old wall was higher partly because this, the oldest part of town, was built on an outcrop of rock above the surrounding marshland, and partly because successive rebuilding on top of the compacted remains of previous structures gradually raised the street level over the centuries. Walk down the steps onto Baldwin Street. At this spot Cabot would have seen a stone cross, and a large stone conduit house. On the other side of the street, the steps continued down to the Avon. In Cabot's day, women did their washing here at high tide, and these steps could also be used to board ships moored alongside. A similar arrangement of doorway and double flight of steps would have been found a little further to the east, at the end of Exchange Avenue (then a continuation of Small Street).

We can now either walk up High Street, to finish our walk where it began, or on to Bristol Bridge for the start of the third walk.

Walk Three

WEAVERS AND WARRIOR MONKS

Beginning at the spot from where Bristol took its name, this walk takes us through the industrial suburbs: Redcliffe and Temple Fee. This area was once a separate township, Bristol's close neighbour and rival, and only became fully part of Bristol with the 1373 charter. We visit the site of a Crusader headquarters, and St Mary Redcliffe, claimed by Bristolians to be the finest parish church in all England.

22) BRISTOL BRIDGE

Standing at the northern end of the bridge, we are close to the origins of Bristol, both the name of the place and the place itself. The name derives from the Saxon word 'Brycgstow', or 'Place by the Bridge', and by the 900s there was a substantial settlement on what is now Castle Park. This site provided an area of raised ground above the surrounding marsh, and the lowest possible bridging point of the Avon; it was also a superb defensive position, with water on three sides, while the long winding approach down the Avon Gorge gave plenty of warning of any attack from the Bristol Channel. The Frome and Avon also provided natural harbours. The first bridge was possibly a little further upstream than the present one. The bridge that Cabot used was carried on four massive stone piers, and had been built during the great period of activity associated with the diversion

of the Frome in the mid-thirteenth century. Like the contemporary London Bridge, it was lined with houses, which projected over the water, supported by great buttresses. These houses were much sought after, perhaps because they were away from the accumulated muck of the town centre (there seems to have been a large refuse mound next to the northern end of the bridge).

In the middle of the bridge was the magnificent chapel of the Assumption of the Virgin Mary, which was finished in 1361 and largely financed by Mayor Elyas Spelley. The chapel stretched across the whole width of the bridge and incorporated a gateway so that the bridge could be sealed off in times of danger. As well as the chapel itself, with its 100-foot tower, the four-storey building contained a number

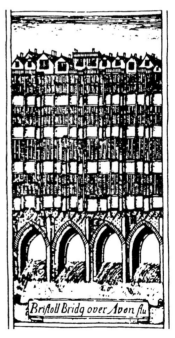

Bristoll Bridg over Avon flu

of chambers, including a hall where the Corporation sometimes met. Also on the bridge were warehouses and public lavatories, known as 'Avon's Privy'.

Looking back to the northern shore, Cabot would have seen, to the right of the bridge, a row of houses and shops called The Shambles (modern Bridge Street). This was where the butchers' shops were. Medieval butchers slaughtered their own meat on the premises, so the riverside location was handy for the disposal of animal waste. Also on this street was another royal customs house: this was a large stone building with three cellars in which wool was kept while it was assessed for duty.

Now cross over the bridge to Victoria Street.

23) ST THOMAS'S CHURCH

Immediately to our left ran Tucker Street. 'Tucker' was the local word for fuller, and we are now entering the cloth-making industrial suburb of Temple Fee and Redcliffe. Excavations on this site promise to reveal a great deal about life and work in Cabot's Bristol. Bearing right along Victoria Street (built in the nineteenth century to provide a thoroughfare to Temple Meads railway station) brings us to St Thomas Street. Here, next to a row of houses built in the fifteenth century, we find St Thomas's church. Most of what we see is late eighteenth century, but the tower would have been familiar to Cabot. Just behind us, in the angle between St Thomas Street and Victoria Street, was Burton's Almshouse. Also nearby in Cabot's day was a stone conduit house.

Walk down St Thomas Lane at the side of the church and cross Redcliffe Street to the riverside (watch for St Mary Redcliffe in the distance). Looking back, we have a fine view of the medieval tower.

24) WELSH BACK

Across the river, the whole length of Welsh Back can be seen. From here operated the coasting trade to Wales and the South West. The bottom of the river channel here is stony and rough, making it dangerous for large vessels to take the ground at low tide, so the ocean-going ships used the Frome, whose bed was softer. Wooden jetties ran along Welsh Back. Standing on this spot, Cabot could have admired the sturdy crane provided by Alice Chestre; this seems to have lifted goods by means of a treadmill, housed in a wooden structure that could be pivoted on a squat post, rather like a windmill. Nearby was Thomas Knapp's chapel, where merchants and sailors could hear mass first thing in the morning before setting out.

Close to Baldwin Street was the Cloth Hall. This had been a luxurious private house, but was given to the Corporation by Robert Sturmy, and by Cabot's day it was used as a meeting place for merchants. The thirteenth-century town wall ran just to the east of King Street, ending at the Marsh Gate beside the Avon. There were two other gates along this stretch of wall, and a ditch in front of it. Beyond the ditch lay the Marsh, a favourite spot for duck hunting. However, this was also the centre of Bristol's ship-building industry: temporary dry docks would be excavated out of the soft ground and then flooded to allow the completed hulls to be floated out onto the river for fitting. No doubt Cabot often walked across the red earth causeway to these shipyards, where he would have seen great iron anchors and the trunks of tall fir trees waiting to be made into masts. He might also have had to watch his step: the Corporation designated the Marsh as one of the few places where rubble, dung and timber could be dumped.

Turn left and continue along the riverside walk as far as the large blue propeller, or screw, mounted in the pavement. Turn left here, pass through the barrier and then turn right along Redcliffe Back, with Buchanan's Wharf to the right.

25) REDCLIFFE BACKS

To the left is a modern housing development, but watch out for two medieval window arches built into the wall ahead. These may be the remains of one of the grandest of Bristol's houses, owned by one of its wealthiest and most famous merchants. William Canynges's mansion stood near here, and behind the main house was a large stone tower with four bay windows. These window arches may have been

part of this tower. We shall see more of what may have been the Canynges House later.

Excavations have told us something of life here in Cabot's day. Much new land had been created along the bank as new docks were built out into the river, and stepped slipways allowed ships to be unloaded at high or low tide. The dyes madder and woad have been found here, as well as home-grown medicinal herbs for the treatment of dysentery and vomiting. That such medicines were needed is suggested by the discovery of rat bones and large numbers of fly pupae; this low-lying, waterside site could not have been very healthy, but wealthy merchants like Canynges were willing to put up with the conditions in order to be close to their business.

Carry on along Redcliffe Backs and cross Redcliffe Way to the gardens on the other side of Redcliffe Hill Road from St Mary's Church.

26) ST MARY REDCLIFFE

We are standing on the site of the Hospital of St John the Baptist. The hospital had been founded by the early thirteenth century. It was the largest of Bristol's almshouses, but was in serious decline in the fifteenth century. A square water conduit stood in the middle of its cloister. In the far wall of the garden is a doorway of late-medieval appearance. This leads into what was a hermit's cell in Cabot's day. On the other side of Redcliffe Hill were two other hospitals, St Mary Magdalene's and St Catherine's, and Canynges's almshouse, served by four priests. St Mary Magdalene's, on the site of the modern General Hospital, was founded in the early thirteenth century for the care of lepers. St Catherine's, founded by the Berkeleys (lords of the manor of Bedminster) in the later thirteenth century, stood near Bedminster Parade.

Cross Redcliffe Hill Road and walk up the steps to St Mary Redcliffe Church. Standing on this spot and looking north, Cabot would have seen the thirteenth-century town wall, the Portwall, with its wide ditch in front, running between the two arms of the Avon: this was the highest and strongest of all the Bristol defensive walls. To the east, where Temple Street meets Portwall Lane, was Temple Gate. This stretch of wall was paid for by the Butchers' Guild. Opposite Temple Gate, just beyond the Portwall ditch, was Magdalene's Almshouse.

Turning back to view St Mary Redcliffe, we see a largely late-medieval structure, but there has been a church on this site since at least the twelfth century. The chapel of the Holy Spirit which stood in the churchyard in Cabot's time may have been the original church before St Mary was built. Technically, this great building was merely a subsidiary church (a 'chapel-of-ease') to the main parish church of St John's in Bedminster; St Mary's grandeur is evidence of the wealth both of the industrial and mercantile suburb of Redcliffe, and of the lords of Berkeley, early patrons of the church. Also in the churchyard was a preaching cross: sermons were given here to the mayor, councillors, and other Bristolians.

The outer north porch of the church was built around 1320, and its exotic detailing seems to have been inspired by oriental art. Perhaps returning crusaders or pilgrims, or merchants trading with Spain, brought back examples of Chinese and Moslem art. Inside the porch is a little side chapel, dedicated to the Virgin Mary: it is said that mariners used to worship here before setting off on their perilous voyages. The room above the porch allowed a priest to keep watch over the chapel, and was later used to store church records.

Within the main body of the church, the north wall at the west end of the nave (above us to the right as we enter the church) shows evidence of rebuilding. This occurred after 1445 or 1446 when a great storm blew down the tower, which crashed into the recently completed church. William Canynges has been credited with financing the rebuilding; while there is little firm evidence to indicate this, his connection with the church is amply demonstrated by his magnificent tombs. These are situated in the south transept. The main tomb, which has been recoloured, shows Canynges with his wife Joan. After Joan's death William became dean of Westbury College, and his other tomb, to the left, depicts him in priestly robes. It is possible that the faces were intended to be likenesses. To the right of the main tomb is an effigy of a fifteenth-century man: a merchant, or perhaps a

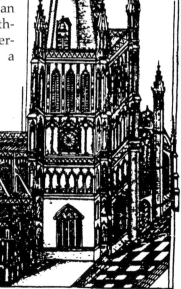

‡ The North prospect of ỹ parrish Church of St Marie Reddiffe in Bristoll

member of Canynges's household. A more certain Canynges connection is provided by the brass set into the floor a few feet from these tombs. This depicts a kitchen knife and colander, and commemorates William Coke, late servant (no doubt in the kitchen) of William Canynges, merchant of Bristol. Another nearby floor memorial is that of John Blecker, who was probably Canynges's brewer.

Other St Mary brasses commemorate John Jay and his wife Joan, the sister of the Bristol antiquary William Worcestre, and their fourteen children; John Juyn, a prominent judge and recorder of Bristol, and John Brook, another judge who died in 1522, and his wife Joanna, a daughter of Richard ap Meryk, or Amerike, who is sometimes supposed to have given his name to the continent that Cabot explored. At the far end of the north choir is the splendid Mede tomb. The effigies probably depict Philip Mede and his wife Isabella, and their son Richard and his two wives Elizabeth and Anne. The Medes had land in Bedminster and elsewhere, and had Bristol mayors and MPs among their number. Another tomb commemorates John Lavyngton, a chantry priest to the chapel of the Holy Spirit in the churchyard. In addition to this, there were as many as twenty-four separate chantries, each with their altars and priests, inside the church. Among these, the best documented were the two founded by William Canynges.

Finally, retracing our steps and entering the 'American Chapel', we see, hanging above the door, a whalebone. This could be our most tangible link to John Cabot, for it is said to have been brought back from his 1497 voyage: alternatively, it is a rib from the monstrous Dun Cow that is supposed to have terrorised Bristol before being slain by the earl of Warwick! After leaving the church, we should note the conduit head built into the churchyard wall on Redcliffe Hill: the water supply was given by Robert, Lord Berkeley, whose twelfth-century tomb is inside the church. Every year in October the vicar and congregation walk the two miles to the conduit's source in Knowle.

Cross Redcliffe Way and walk to the junction of Portwall Lane and Redcliffe Street.

27) REDCLIFFE STREET

Redcliffe Gate stood here in Cabot's time. Just outside the gate was another conduit. Immediately inside the gate, on the right-hand side of Redcliffe Street, was the almshouse of Richard Foster. A little further up, on the opposite side of the road, is a modern block of flats with an adjoining courtyard. Looking through the gate, we can see a stone arcade running west from the road. This is the other survival of the large medieval house whose remains we first encountered on Redcliffe Backs, and which may have belonged to William Canynges. This part of the house was only demolished in 1937. The arcade ran along the north side of the hall, which was immediately behind the street range. Remnants of a stone piscina, or wash basin, survive in the arcade. The hall had a magnificent wooden roof. Beyond the hall was a large chamber, which may have been where Canynges entertained Edward IV in 1461. A fine pavement has been removed from the site and is now in the British Museum. Two courtyards separated the main house from the stone tower on Redcliffe Backs.

Canynges lived in the heart of an industrial suburb. Archaeologists have found evidence of weaving, dye works, shoemaking, tanneries, baking, and metalworking, including moulds for forging bells or dye vats. An igloo-shaped stone building excavated just inside Redcliffe Gate was probably a baker's oven. Redcliffe St was also the home of painters: pigments of blue from copper ore and red from lead have been found here, together with oyster shells, perhaps used as palettes. Redcliffe Hill once had flourishing potteries, but by Cabot's day these were being forced out of business by competition from Malvern and north Wiltshire potters.

Turn right into Three Queens' Lane, cross St Thomas Street into Mitchell Lane and stop at the junction of Victoria Street and Temple Street.

28) TEMPLE CHURCH

We have just crossed the two 'law ditches' that ran between and parallel to Redcliffe, St Thomas Street and Temple Street. They drained these low-lying, marshy areas and fed into the Portwall ditch. Looking right down Temple Street towards Portwall, Cabot would have seen, a little way down the road on his left, Weavers' Hall, a two-storeyed structure, with the hall itself on the first floor and the weavers' almshouse underneath. Built at the end of the thirteenth century, this was the oldest purpose-built guild hall in Bristol. At the end of Temple Street, just inside Temple Gate and to the right of the road was Spicer's almshouse, probably founded by John Spicer, mayor of Bristol, in 1352. The almshouse was rebuilt in the later fifteenth century, and the site has been excavated. Opposite Spicer's Almshouse was the Augustinian Friary, the fourth and last of Bristol's friaries, founded in 1313. Over the three years before its suppression in 1538, the prior sold off the plate and timber that grew in the friary grounds.

Turn around, head north up Temple Street and through the gate to Temple Church. Temple Church, dedicated to the Holy Cross, is largely a late-fourteenth-century structure, but the original church on this site was part of the preceptory, or regional headquarters, for the Knights Templars, an order of crusading warrior monks. Their original purpose was to help free the Holy Land from Moslem domination, but they received so many gifts of land throughout Christian Europe that they became virtually a multi-national corporation. Their vast wealth eventually brought about their downfall, since in the early fourteenth century the king of France, in an effort to get his hands on their fortune, persuaded the pope to suppress the order and their leaders were burnt at the stake on charges of heresy, witchcraft and sexual misconduct. One of their benefactors was Robert earl of Gloucester, who in the mid-twelfth century gave them the eastern marshland in the bend of the Avon. This became known as Temple Fee (Temple Meads has the same origin). The Templars built one of their characteristic circular churches on this site (circular in imitation of the 'Temple of Solomon' in Jerusalem, from which they took their name). Between 1309 and 1312, after their suppression, the site was taken over by another crusading order, the Knights of St John, or Hospitallers. The circular Templar church was demolished, and the present structure built in its place, as the parish church of the industrial suburb of Temple Fee, which had grown up on the drained marshland. When the English Hospitallers were suppressed during the Dissolution, Bristol Corporation bought their property in Temple Fee.

The tower leans because of the marshy foundations on which it was built. The upper stage of the tower was built in the mid-fifteenth century. By then the tower was already leaning, since the decoration of the upper stage is at a different angle to that lower down. New bells were hung in the 1460s (perhaps cast in pits dug in the churchyard and uncovered by archaeologists), and when they were rung the tower shook alarmingly, and a crack appeared between the tower and the body of the church. In the sixteenth century a stone the size of an ostrich egg was placed in this crack and was crushed as the bells sounded. The Hospitallers built a large hall to the north of the church, and adjoining this was the vicarage. The discovery here of fourteenth-century tiles bearing the Berkeley arms shows that the family was still influential. The church was bombed in 1940.

Now we leave the churchyard and turn right, back onto Temple Street, which we follow northwards.

29) TEMPLE STREET

This had once been one of the busiest streets in Bristol, the centre of the town's cloth industry. But by Cabot's day the street's wool-carding, weaving and fulling industries were in decline. Just above Water Lane was the Neptune Conduit, and close by was the Tuckers' Hall. Like the weavers, the tuckers (or fullers) incorporated an almshouse or hospital below their guildhall. Even in this centre of industry, there was still room for flower and herb gardens, whose remains have been detected by archaeologists.

At the crossroads formed by Temple Street and Countess Passage was the Stallage Cross, where Temple Street Market was held. Stalls were set up around the Stallage Cross: 'stallage' was the fee paid by the traders for setting up their stalls.

Turning right into Counterslip Passage brings us to Temple Back, and the river. Cabot would have known Counterslip Passage as the Countess's Slip, perhaps named after the countess of Gloucester, in memory of an aristocratic family whose influence over Bristol had once been as great as that of the

Berkeleys. For Cabot, the passage would have led down to a slip, or steps leading down to the river. We cross the river by St Philip's Bridge, but before this was built, a ferry plied between the two banks of the Avon here. Taking the ferry from the Countess Slip, Cabot could have admired the castle walls to his left, while to his right the open ground behind Temple Back would have been scattered with wooden frames, the racks on which cloth was left to dry, 'on tenterhooks'. Beyond, rising up in the distance, was the Harratz Tower, the huge round tower that stood at the end of the Portwall (roughly where Temple Way now crosses the river). Recent excavations have uncovered its massive foundations.

Continuing along Counterslip Passage brings us to the churchyard of Saints Philip and James.

30) THE CHURCH OF SAINTS PHILIP AND JAMES AND OLD MARKET

Narrow and Broad Plain and Unity Street probably follow the line of the bank and ditch that in Cabot's time curved around this eastern suburb of Bristol as far as the Frome on the north side.

The exterior of the church of Saints Philip and James would be instantly recognisable by Cabot, but the interior was largely remodelled in the eighteenth century. A Benedictine priory may once have stood on this site, but by the fifteenth century this parish church had been built to serve the area around Old Market Street. This street, now rudely interrupted by the Bond Street/Temple Way roundabout, was known as Old Market even in Cabot's day, and its growth was probably stimulated by the needs of the garrison in the Castle's heyday. It was also the beginning of the main Bristol to London road, and kings such as Edward IV and Henry VII came this way on their visits to the town. Its width (it is recorded as being 108 feet wide in the fifteenth century) allowed for market stalls to be ranged down the middle of the road, a common arrangement in medieval market towns.

A gate and bridge connected the west end of Old Market with the Castle, and here stood the market cross. Another cross, the Red Cross, stood near the junction of modern Redcross Street and Asher Lane. Beyond the houses either side of Old Market lay orchards and gardens. The Stag and Hounds, on the corner of Old Market and Temple Way, contains medieval remains, and was the site of the Pie Powder Court, where market disputes were settled. In Cabot's day this would have taken place under one of the arcades that lined the street (similar to the Tolzeys on Corn Street). Some arcades can still be seen, but none are medieval. At the far end of Old

Market was Lafford's (Lawford's) Gate, built to allow access through the defensive bank and ditch that enclosed this end of town. Just inside the gate was Trinity Hospital, founded by a local merchant called John Barstaple for thirteen poor men. Barstaple died in 1410 and he is buried in the hospital chapel with his wife Isabel. The present hospital is a nineteenth-century rebuilding, by the same architects who rebuilt Foster's Almshouse. Beyond the gate was the leper hospital of St Lawrence. It was founded by Prince (later King) John, but by the early fifteenth century it was in decay, with only four almsfolk, and in 1465 it was taken over by Westbury College.

Our tour of Cabot's Bristol ends here. It's quite a walk back to Bristol Bridge, but there are plenty of buses along Temple Way!

FURTHER READING

CABOT AND EXPLORATION

P. McGrath, 'Bristol and America, 1480–1631', in K.R. Andrews et al. (eds), *The Westward Enterprise* (1978), reprinted as a Bristol Historical Association pamphlet, 1997.

D.B. Quinn, *Sebastian Cabot and Bristol Exploration*, Bristol Historical Association (1993).

I. Wilson, *The Columbus Myth* (1992).

I. Wilson, *John Cabot and the Matthew* (1996).

GENERAL ACCOUNTS OF BRISTOL

A.L. Beetham-Fisher, 'The Merchants of Medieval Bristol, 1350–1500', University of Oregon Ph.D. thesis (1987) (copy in Bristol Record Office).

P.W. Fleming, 'The Emergence of Modern Bristol', in M. Dresser and P. Ollerenshaw (eds), *The Making of Modern Bristol* (1996).

B. Little, *The City and County of Bristol* (1954).

B. Little, *The Story of Bristol* (1991).

D.M. Lobel and E.M. Carus-Wilson, *Historic Towns: Bristol* (1975).

C.M. McInnes and W.E.Whittard (eds), *Bristol and its Adjoining Counties* (1955).

M. Manson, *Bristol Beyond the Bridge* (1988).

D.H. Sacks, 'Trade, Society and Politics in Bristol, c. 1500–c. 1640', University of Harvard Ph.D. thesis (1977) (copy in Bristol Record Office).

D.H. Sacks, *The Widening Gate: Bristol and the Atlantic Economy, 1450–1700* (1991).

B.S. Smith and E. Ralph, *A History of Bristol and Gloucestershire* (second edition, 1996).

For modern editions of original Bristol records, see:

F.B. Bickley (ed), *The Little Red Book of Bristol* (1900).

E. Ralph (ed), *The Great White Book of Bristol*, Bristol Record Society, volume 32 (1979).

L. Toulmin Smith (ed), *The Maire of Bristowe is Kalendar, by Robert Ricart, Town Clerk of Bristol*, Camden Society (1872).

E.W.W. Veale (ed), *The Great Red Book of Bristol*, Bristol Record Society, volumes 2, 4, 8, 16 (1933–53).

CLOTH AND CANVAS

A. Crawford, *Bristol and the Wine Trade*, Bristol Historical Association (1984).

J.W. Sherborne, *The Port of Bristol in the Middle Ages*, Bristol Historical Association (1965).

J. Vanes, *The Port of Bristol in the Sixteenth Century*, Bristol Historical Association (1977).

For modern editions of original Bristol records see:

E.M. Carus Wilson (ed), *The Overseas Trade of Bristol in the Later Middle Ages*, Bristol Record Society, volume 7 (1937).

J. Vanes (ed), *Documents Illustrating the Overseas Trade of Bristol in the Sixteenth Century*, Bristol Record Society, volume 31 (1979).

CROWNS AND CHARTERS

E. Ralph, *The Government of Bristol, 1373-1973* (1973).

For modern editions of Bristol charters see:

H.A. Cronne (ed), *Bristol Charters, 1378–1499*, Bristol Record Society, volume 11 (1946).

N.D. Harding (ed), *Bristol Charters, 1155–1373*, Bristol Record Society, volume 1 (1930).

R.C. Latham (ed), *Bristol Charters, 1509–1899*, Bristol Record Society, volume 12 (1947).

PAUPERS AND MERCHANT PRINCES

E. Ralph, *The Streets of Bristol*, Bristol Historical Association (1981).

J.W. Sherborne, *William Canynges, 1402–1474*, Bristol Historical Association (1985).

J. Vanes, *Education and Apprenticeship in Sixteenth-Century Bristol*, Bristol Historical Association (1982).

T.P. Wadley, *Notes or Abstracts of the Wills contained in ... the Great Orphans' Book and Book of Wills* (1886).

PRIESTS AND PULPITS

J.H. Bettey, *Bristol Parish Churches during the Reformation, c. 1530–1560*, Bristol Historical Association (1979).

C. Burgess, '"By Quick and by Dead": Wills and Pious Provision in Late Medieval Bristol', *English Historical Review*, volume 102 (1987).

C. Burgess, 'A Service for the Dead: the Form and Function of the Anniversary in Late Medieval Bristol', *Transactions of the Bristol and Gloucestershire Archaeological Society*, volume 105 (1987).

C. Burgess, *The Parish Church and the Laity in Late Medieval Bristol*, Bristol Historical Association (1992).

N. Orme, 'The Guild of Kalendars, Bristol', *Transactions of the Bristol and Gloucestershire Archaeological Society*, volume 96 (1978).

E. Ralph and J. Rogan (eds), *Essays in Cathedral History* (1991).

M. Skeeters, *Community and Clergy: Bristol and the Reformation, c. 1530–c. 1570* (1993).

M.Q. Smith, *The Medieval Churches of Bristol*, Bristol Historical Association (1970).

For modern editions of Bristol ecclesiastical records, see:

C. Burgess (ed), *The Pre-Reformation Records of All Saints', Bristol: Part One*, Bristol Record Society, volume 46 (1995).

B.R. Masters and E. Ralph (eds), *The Church Book of St Ewens* (1967).

C. Ross (ed), *The Cartulary of St Mark's Hospital*, Bristol Record Society, volume 21 (1956).

See also the registers of the bishops of Bath and Wells published by the Somerset Record Society, volumes 29-32, 52, 54-5 (1914–1940).

WALKING CABOT'S BRISTOL

E.J. Boore, *Excavations at Tower Lane, Bristol* (1984).

J. Dallaway, *Antiquities of Bristow in the Middle Centuries* (1834) (for William Worcestre's survey).

R.H. Jones, *Excavations in Redcliffe, 1983–5* (1986).

R. Leech, *The Topography of Medieval and Early-Modern Bristol: Part One*, Bristol Record Society, volume 47 (1997).

M. Ponsford, *Excavations at Greyfriars, Bristol* (1975).

R. Price, *Excavations at St Bartholomew's Hospital, Bristol* (1979).

S. Watson, *Secret Underground Bristol* (1991).

L. Watts and P. Rahtz, *Mary-le-Port, Bristol: Excavations, 1962–3* (1985).

B. Williams, *Excavations in the Medieval Suburb of Redcliffe, Bristol, 1980* (1981).

For other archaeological reports, see the journals *Transactions of the Bristol and Gloucestershire Archaeological Society* and *Bristol and Avon Archaeology*. For further references to Bristol archaeology, see N. Dixon, *An Archaeological Bibliography of Bristol* (1987), and J. Brett, *An Historical and Archaeological Bibliography of Bristol, 1987–1994* (1995). Also, the Bristol Database Project, based at the Faculty of Humanities, University of the West of England (St Matthias Campus), has produced a bibliography of Bristol history in computer-readable formats.